Contents

Introduction

Chronology provides a fundamental structure for our understanding of the past. Timing reveals the sequence of past events and the tempo of change, and provides a window on human temporality. Scientific dating enables us to provide increasingly refined chronological frameworks for the historic environment, enhancing understanding and appreciation of its value and significance, informing conservation and protection, and enthusing the public about their heritage.

Constructing robust chronologies requires rigour at all stages of the dating programme. Bayesian statistics provide an explicit methodology for combining different strands of information to provide such a chronology. They have proven particularly valuable in handling the complex probability distributions of calibrated radiocarbon dates, but it is also possible to include dates from coins, historical sources, dendrochronology and the results of other scientific dating methods such as luminescence and archaeomagnetic dating. A scientific dating programme undertaken within a Bayesian framework should thus be the norm, not the exception.

Radiocarbon dating is applicable to an extensive range of materials that commonly survive in archaeological sites, historic buildings and palaeoenvironmental records. It can be used for samples up to *c.* 50,000 years old.

It is widely available on a commercial basis, and measurement error compares favourably with many other techniques. It is thus the scientific dating technique most commonly used to understand heritage assets, although its complexities raise formidable challenges in constructing robust and precise chronologies.

This guidance is designed to lead the reader through the Bayesian process that should be at the heart of all scientific dating programmes. It aims to provide the non-specialist reader with the necessary information to employ radiocarbon dating appropriately, and to be aware of the scientific and statistical complexities that can arise and require specialist support.

This document is intended for:

■ curators who advise local planning authorities and issue briefs;

■ project managers writing specifications or written schemes of investigation;

■ those working on development-led or research projects (in particular post-excavation project managers);

■ other practitioners.

These guidelines are designed to be relevant to archaeological projects funded under the planning process within England. They concentrate on using radiocarbon dating and chronological modelling within the Holocene Period. Specialist advice should be sought when dating earlier sites (guidance on dating techniques for the Pleistocene Period is currently in preparation).

Although the general principles of these guidelines are widely applicable, there are some technical aspects of radiocarbon dating that are not covered in this document, as they are not usually relevant for English sites. Such issues include, for example, the dating of marine shell. Very little information will also be found on materials that are dated only rarely (for example, chitin), and again specialist advice should be sought before submitting such materials for dating.

An introduction to the methods is provided in §1 and §2, covering radiocarbon dating and Bayesian Chronological Modelling. A step-by-step guide to the practice of implementing a radiocarbon dating programme is provided in §3 (and summarised in Fig. 11), including a series of flow-diagrams to aid readers through various stages of the process (Figs 18–21, 23 and 25). Project management within the English planning framework is discussed in §4 and a range of case studies is provided in §5. A glossary is provided for less familiar terms (highlighted in bold in the text), and an appendix details sources of further advice, information and resources.

Radiocarbon dating

1.1 Fundamental principles

Radiocarbon (^{14}C) is a naturally occurring radioactive **isotope** of carbon that is formed in the upper atmosphere when neutrons produced by cosmic rays interact with nitrogen atoms (Fig. 1). It is unstable, with a physical **half-life** of 5730±40 years.

Once produced, radiocarbon atoms rapidly oxidise to form carbon dioxide (CO_2) that disperses quickly within the atmosphere and enters the terrestrial food chain through photosynthesis. This means that the ^{14}C content of plants that live on land, and the animals that eat the plants, is in equilibrium with the contemporary atmosphere. When an organism dies it ceases to take up radiocarbon,

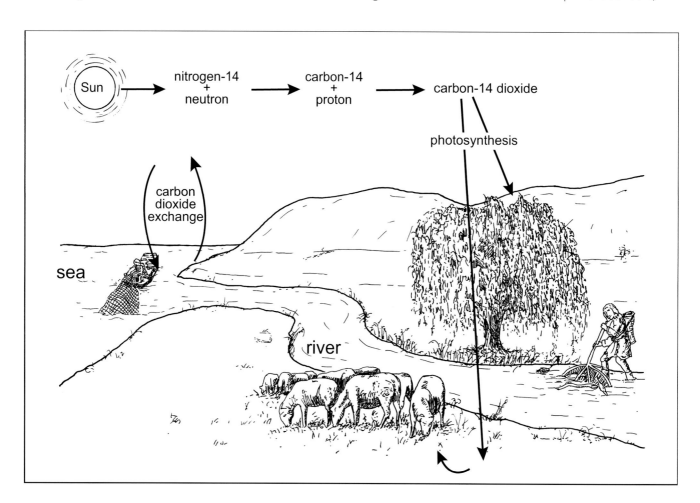

Figure 1: The carbon cycle: ^{14}C is formed in the upper atmosphere by the interaction of neutrons from cosmic rays with ^{14}N. This is absorbed very quickly into the terrestrial biosphere through photosynthesis and the ingestion of plants by animals. Absorption of atmospheric ^{14}C into the marine environment, and some other reservoirs, is slower and it can be diluted by carbon from other sources, often leading to an age-offset between contemporary samples from different biospheres (image by I. Dennis).

and so over time, due to natural **radioactive decay**, the proportion of ^{14}C in the dead organism decreases. By measuring the proportion that remains, the elapsed time since death can be estimated. The age can be calculated from the ratio of ^{14}C in the material of unknown age to that in a modern standard, using the exponential formula for radiocarbon decay (Bowman 1990, 11).

Radiocarbon enters other reservoirs more slowly or, once there, is diluted by a component of ^{14}C-free carbon. For example, the ocean surface is on average 400 radiocarbon years older than the contemporary atmosphere, although regional up-welling of deep water can make offsets in some areas much larger than this. Freshwater offsets in rivers and lakes are extremely variable and need to be measured locally.

Any organic material that was once alive can be dated using radiocarbon (e.g. bones, seeds, wood, shell), as can some materials that absorb carbon during their manufacture (e.g. lime mortar, steel). Further information on the principles of radiocarbon dating and the carbon cycle can be found in Bowman (1990) or Walker (2012).

1.2 Measuring radiocarbon

The procedures used for the preparation and dating of samples in the laboratory are critical for accurate radiocarbon dating. Radiocarbon is very difficult to measure, in large part because the ^{14}C concentration in living material is extremely low (about 1 in every 1 million million carbon atoms). This makes detecting a radiocarbon atom in a sample at the limit of detection (*c.* 50,000 years old) equivalent to identifying a single specific human hair that might occur on the head of any of the human beings alive on earth today!

During the past 60 years, techniques for purification of samples and measurement of radiocarbon have developed. There are, however, steps common to all methods of radiocarbon dating (Fig. 2).

To date an archaeological sample accurately, it is essential that only the ^{14}C that was part of the organism when it died is measured. Therefore, the first task is to pretreat the sample effectively to remove any exogenous carbon that has entered the sample since death. This contamination usually comes from the burial environment, but can also come from such things as inappropriate packaging or the conservation procedures that an object may have undergone. **Pretreatment** includes a mixture of physical and chemical processes, and varies both according to the type of material being processed and the laboratory undertaking the analysis. The outcome is a contaminant-free chemical fraction of a sample that can be dated.

There are fundamentally two ways of measuring the amount of radiocarbon in a sample.

Until the mid-1980s all radiocarbon dating was undertaken using conventional techniques, which count the decay of ^{14}C atoms using either

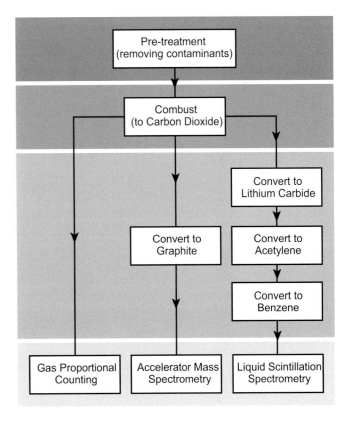

Figure 2: An overview of methods for measuring radiocarbon in archaeological samples (image by J. Vallender).

gas proportional counting or **liquid scintillation spectrometry**. Respectively, these techniques involve converting the purified sample into either a gas (e.g. carbon dioxide) or a carbon-rich aromatic liquid (e.g. benzene), and then measuring **β-particles** emitted by the radioactive decay of ${}^{14}C$. While conventional dating methods can be extremely precise and accurate, they require large samples (e.g. 200g of bone) and usually require long processing and counting times taking several months.

Nowadays, **Accelerator Mass Spectrometry (AMS)** is almost always used for measuring the amount of radiocarbon in samples. This enables much smaller samples to be dated (e.g. 1g of bone). Typically, a sample is combusted to carbon dioxide and then converted to graphite (Fig. 3). This is pressed into a target that is loaded into the accelerator. In the AMS carbon atoms are given a specific electric charge and accelerated to very high speeds, which allows the three carbon isotopes (${}^{12}C$, ${}^{13}C$ and ${}^{14}C$) to be separated by mass using one or more powerful magnets. The methods used for combustion, graphitisation and dating vary according to both the equipment available and the laboratory undertaking the analysis.

Further information on the methods used for radiocarbon dating can be found in Bayliss et al. (2004) or Taylor and Bar-Yosef (2014, chapter 4).

1.3 Radiocarbon results

Most radiocarbon results obtained for archaeological projects are reported as conventional radiocarbon ages measured on the radiocarbon timescale in units 'BP'. This reflects the concentration of radiocarbon in a sample (with 0 BP defined as the radiocarbon concentration in AD 1950). Such ages have been calculated using standards that have been internationally agreed (Stuiver and Polach 1977), and have been calculated in a way that allows for improvements in our understanding of the half-life of radiocarbon and for fractionation (*see* §1.4). They provide a

Figure 3: Combusting a sample to carbon dioxide, before its conversion into graphite for measurement by Accelerator Mass Spectrometry (photograph by H. Granlund Marsden).

common standard for users of radiocarbon dating and should be published in preference to other forms of radiocarbon result that may be reported (e.g. measured radiocarbon ages, which are not corrected for fractionation). There are three essential components to each measurement: the unique laboratory identifier, the **conventional radiocarbon age** and the error estimate (e.g. Beta-194560, 3630±30 BP). By convention, error estimates are reported at 1σ. Samples that date to beyond the limit of radiocarbon dating will be reported as beyond the background detection limit of the facility concerned (e.g. GrA-32659, > 45,000 BP).

Some samples may date to after AD 1950. The radiocarbon content of these samples is expressed as a fraction of modern carbon (Mook and van der Plicht 1999). Again, there are three essential components to the measurement: the unique laboratory identifier, the fraction modern value and the error estimate (e.g. SUERC-6782, 1.0300±0.0047 $F^{14}C$). The fraction modern value should be reported in preference to other forms of result that may be reported (e.g. percent modern carbon, PMC).

Sometimes replicate ages may be obtained by dating a sample more than once. In these cases, the statistical consistency of the results can be assessed using the method of Ward and Wilson (1978), and consistent groups of ages combined before calibration by taking a **weighted mean**. For example, carbonised residue on the interior of an Iron Age vessel from Beckford, Worcestershire, provided two radiocarbon ages from different laboratories (OxA-16776, 2296±28 BP and GrA-33519, 2235±35 BP), which are statistically consistent (T'=1.8; T'(5%)=3.8; df=1), and so a weighted mean can be calculated (2272±22 BP). This approach is only valid for groups of radiocarbon determinations that are true replicates — that is repeat measurements on the same sample or organism. Alternative statistical approaches are available for other situations where we have groups of measurements that are related in other ways (*see* §2.2).

1.4 Fractionation and δ¹³C values

Fractionation occurs when the heavier carbon isotopes, ¹³C and ¹⁴C, are processed in a different way to the lighter ¹²C isotope during certain physical, chemical or biological processes. It occurs both in nature and during the laboratory processing of a radiocarbon sample. For example, during photosynthesis the lighter isotopes are kinetically favoured and so are taken up preferentially. This means that the parts of a growing plant that are still exchanging CO_2 with the atmosphere will have a lower ¹⁴C concentration than the air, and will produce a date that is too old unless a correction is applied for fractionation. Physical processes can discriminate against either heavier or lighter isotopes. Such fractionation in the laboratory is most common in the combustion stage of conventional dating, and in the graphitisation and measurement stages of AMS.

Fortunately, ¹³C and ¹²C are **stable isotopes** and so the ¹³C /¹²C ratio in a sample remains constant over time and can be measured. This is the δ¹³C value, which is the difference, in parts per thousand (per mille, ‰), between the ratio of ¹³C to ¹²C in the sample and the ratio of ¹³C to ¹²C in an internationally agreed standard. The δ¹³C can be used to estimate the original ¹⁴C :¹²C ratio in a sample, because the effect of fractionation on the ¹⁴C:¹²C ratio is approximately double that for the ¹³C:¹²C ratio, reflecting the mass difference between the heavier isotopes and ¹²C.

The δ¹³C values provided by radiocarbon laboratories are of interest to users of radiocarbon dating for three reasons:

First, they can be used to correct fractionation in the measured ¹⁴C concentration and to calculate a conventional radiocarbon age. The conventional radiocarbon age of an enriched sample (with a less negative δ¹³C value than the −25.0‰ to which all conventional radiocarbon ages are normalised) is greater (older) than its measured radiocarbon age. Correction for isotopic fractionation in a depleted sample (with a more negative δ¹³C value) gives a lower (younger) conventional radiocarbon age. A difference of 1‰ in δ¹³C corresponds to a ¹⁴C age difference of *c.* 16 BP.

Material	$\delta^{13}C$ value
wood, peat, & C³ plants	−25‰
bone collagen	−19‰
calcined bone	n/a
freshwater plants	−16‰
freshwater fish	−22‰
marine plants	−12‰
marine fish	−14‰
marine mammals	−14‰

Table 1: Typical $\delta^{13}C$ values for various materials. Note that these can vary by ±2‰ or ±3‰ (and that a difference of 1‰ equates to a difference of *c.* 16 BP in age calculation).

Ideally, all conventional radiocarbon ages should be calculated using a measured $\delta^{13}C$ value. Occasionally, samples are too small to enable a measurement of $\delta^{13}C$ as well as the radiocarbon content, and in the past not all radiocarbon facilities had access to the equipment needed to measure $\delta^{13}C$. In these cases, an assumed value based on typical values for different types of material can be used for age calculation (Table 1). This is, however, not ideal, particularly as the precision of measurements improves, and so for archaeological samples, measured $\delta^{13}C$ values should be obtained whenever possible.

The second use of $\delta^{13}C$ values for archaeologists is to check for samples whose carbon is not derived fully from atmospheric or terrestrial sources, and so could have **reservoir** effects that have to be considered during the **calibration** process (*see* §1.6). Again, $\delta^{13}C$ values measured by conventional mass spectrometry that are more than a few per mille away from the typical values listed in Table 1 should invoke caution. For example, a bulk sediment sample from the base of Askham Bog, Yorkshire, produced a measurement of 9150±55BP (OxA-8262) with a $\delta^{13}C$ value of −15.0‰, which suggests that this sample may have a significant **hard-water error**. Potentially, such enriched carbon isotopic values in human bone or food

residues from pottery can indicate samples with a strong input of marine resources. Examples such as these from England, however, are rare.

More common are samples from humans who have ingested a modest component of marine or freshwater fish in their diets (< 20%). This can be indicated by only slightly elevated $\delta^{13}C$ values (> −19.0‰), and further isotopic studies would be required to estimate the proportion of such resources consumed (*see* §5.2). The significance of diet-induced reservoir offsets of this scale depends on the precision and accuracy required from the specific application.

The third use of $\delta^{13}C$ values for archaeologists is as a quality check on the radiocarbon age. For this purpose, it is essential to determine how the quoted $\delta^{13}C$ value has been obtained. Basically, there are two ways of measuring $\delta^{13}C$. In many accelerators, it can be measured on-line during the dating process. In this case, the measurement includes the natural isotopic composition of the sample, but also all the fractionation that may have occurred during laboratory processing and AMS measurement. Values of this kind are normally reported as '$\delta^{13}C_{AMS}$'. It is also possible to measure $\delta^{13}C$ by conventional Isotopic Ratio Mass Spectrometry (IRMS), as is done for stable isotopic studies. Values of this kind are normally reported as '$\delta^{13}C_{IRMS}$'. In this case, either the collagen extracted for dating or the carbon dioxide produced by the combustion process is sub-sampled. For AMS measurements, where closed-system combustion is employed, the resultant value largely relates to the natural isotopic composition of the sample; but for conventional dating, where open-tube combustion is used, the reported $\delta^{13}C$ value will include both the natural isotopic composition of the sample and any fractionation that has occurred during combustion (and so again these measurements do not necessarily reflect the natural isotopic composition of the sample).

Unfortunately, at present there is no consensus among radiocarbon laboratories about how $\delta^{13}C$ is measured and about which values are reported to users. Some laboratories use $\delta^{13}C$ values measured on the AMS to calculate ages, and report those values (e.g. ETH-, KIA-) or do not report these values (Poz-); some laboratories use $\delta^{13}C$ values measured by conventional mass spectrometry to calculate ages, and report those values (e.g. SUERC-); some laboratories use $\delta^{13}C$ values measured on the AMS to calculate ages, but report a second $\delta^{13}C$ value on the same sample measured by conventional mass spectrometry (e.g. OxA-, GrM-). Consequently, it is necessary to ask your chosen facility:

1   how the $\delta^{13}C$ value that has been used to calculate the reported conventional radiocarbon age has been measured, and

2   how the $\delta^{13}C$ value that has been reported to you has been measured.

This is important because the utility of a $\delta^{13}C$ value for quality assurance of radiocarbon dates for users of radiocarbon dating depends on how it has been measured. Values measured by AMS are of great worth for the calculation of accurate conventional radiocarbon ages, but can vary appreciably from the typical values listed in Table 1 without affecting the quality of the resultant age. Values measured by conventional mass spectrometry usually lie within a few per mille of the typical values listed in Table 1. Where they do not, there is possibly either a contamination issue with the sample or a problem with the measurement process, either of which merits further consideration.

For example, a crouched burial at Mile Oak, Sussex produced a radiocarbon age of 2240±70 BP (GU-5269), with a $\delta^{13}C$ value measured by conventional mass spectrometry of −26.4‰. This is notably depleted for a sample of bone collagen (Table 1) and so the skeleton was re-dated, producing two statistically consistent ages, both of which are significantly earlier than GU-5269 (GU-5675, 2810 ±70 BP and GU-5691, 2960±100 BP) and have $\delta^{13}C$ values within the expected range (−20.5‰ and −22.9‰). It seems probable that the original measurement was in error.

Key facts: radiocarbon results and $\delta^{13}C$ values

There are three components to a radiocarbon result:

■   the unique laboratory identifier (e.g. Beta- or SUERC-)

■   conventional radiocarbon age (e.g. 3630 BP) or fraction modern value (e.g. 1.0300 F^{14}C)

■   the experimental uncertainty at 1σ (e.g. ±30 BP or ±0.0047 F^{14}C)

Replicate measurements on the same sample or organism should be combined by taking a weighted mean before calibration.

$\delta^{13}C$ values are necessary to account for fractionation in radiocarbon dating. Those measured by AMS ($\delta^{13}C_{AMS}$) are used in age calculation; those measured by IRMS ($\delta^{13}C_{IRMS}$) may be used in age calculation, but may also be used to identify potential reservoir effects and as a measure of quality control.

1.5 Calibration

Calibration is an essential step in using radiocarbon measurements to estimate the calendar date of samples. It is necessary because the production rate of radiocarbon in the atmosphere is not constant, but varies through time. This means that we need to convert the radiocarbon measurement of a sample to the calendar scale using a calibration curve made up of radiocarbon ages measured on samples of known calendar date.

Calibrated dates must be accompanied by a statement of the calibration curve and method used for their calculation and, if appropriate, details of any reservoir correction applied.

Calibrated radiocarbon dates are usually cited at 95% probability, but the 68% probability is also often provided. In some circumstances, 99% probability is more appropriate. In English archaeology, calibrated dates are usually given on the historical cal BC/cal AD scale, although the cal BP scale (measured from AD 1950) is common in the palaeoenvironmental literature.

Fortunately, there is now a set of internationally agreed consensus calibration curves for the whole timescale covered by the radiocarbon method. These should be used for all applications. Those relevant to England are:

- the terrestrial calibration curve for the mid-latitude northern hemisphere (IntCal20; Reimer et al. 2020)

- the atmospheric calibration curve for samples from the northern hemisphere zone 1 dating to after AD 1950 (bomb21NH1; Hua et al. 2021)

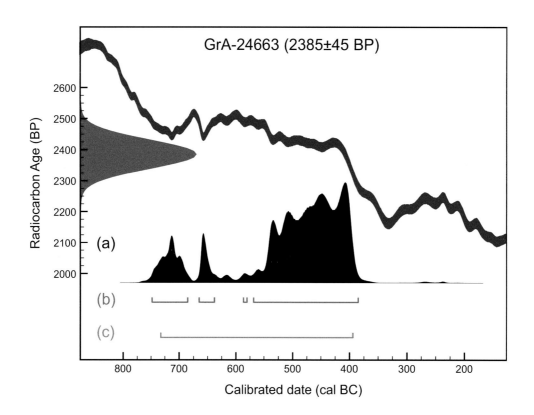

Figure 4: Calibration of a radiocarbon age (image by A. Bayliss):

(a) the probability method converts the probability distribution of the radiocarbon age (in red) to the calendar scale through the calibration curve (in blue) to produce a probability distribution of the calibrated radiocarbon date (in black);

(b) the probability method calculates the minimum number of discrete ranges needed to describe a given amount of probability from the distribution (illustrated at 95%). These ranges are shown in red below the probability distribution of the calibrated date in Figure 4b. So, for example, GrA-24663 dates to 749–685 cal BC (11% probability) or 666–638 cal BC (5% probability) or 567–385 cal BC (79% probability), which together describe 95% of the probability in the calibrated distribution, giving us a 1 in 20 chance that the true date of this sample lies outside one of these ranges;

(c) The quantile range calculates the continuous range that includes a given amount of probability from the distribution (illustrated at 95%). This range is shown in green below the probability distribution of the calibrated date in Figure 4c. So, for example, GrA-24663 dates to 734–395 cal BC (95% probability).

- the hypothetical 'global' marine reservoir (Marine20; Heaton et al. 2020), which has to be modified to reflect local surface water using location-specific corrections (*see* §1.6).

Radiocarbon calibration is an active area of research, and these curves are refined and updated periodically. It is thus certain that radiocarbon measurements will need to be re-calibrated in due course, and so it is essential that both the unique laboratory identifier and the uncalibrated radiocarbon age and error are cited in publication in addition to the calibrated radiocarbon date (*see* §3.6.1).

Bayesian Chronological Modelling provides date estimates that include the calibration process, and so single-sample calibration is not required for applications where modelling is employed.

Calibration is usually undertaken using the probability method (Stuiver and Reimer 1993) illustrated in Figure 4. This is where the probability distribution of the radiocarbon age (in red; Fig. 4a) is converted to the calendar scale through the calibration curve to produce a probability distribution of the calibrated radiocarbon date (in black). This distribution is the most accurate reflection of the full complexity of the calendar date of a sample and is used when further statistical modelling is undertaken (*see* §2). In discussion, however, this distribution needs to be summarised. As illustrated in Figure 4b, the probability method usually produces several date ranges, all of which, however, are needed to summarise the probability distribution of the calibrated date adequately. This can be awkward.

For this reason, quantile ranges can be quoted (Fig. 4c). These always provide a single, continuous date range that is easy to cite in publication and has a known probability (again 95% probability or 68% probability is usually employed). The disadvantage of this summary is that it does not reflect the full complexities of the calibrated radiocarbon date. This possibly

does not matter if, for example, the measurement is providing a range-finder date for a deposit or structure (*see* §2.1).

As in any scientific process, at the last stage of analysis, results should be rounded to avoid false precision. Calibrated radiocarbon date ranges should be rounded outwards, to a resolution that is dependent on that of the calibration curve used and the radiocarbon age that is being calibrated (Fig. 5).

Using IntCal20, results that calibrate after cal AD 1950, should be rounded outwards to one year (Fig. 5a); results with error terms less than ±25 BP that calibrate between cal AD 1950 and cal AD 1000 should also be calibrated outwards to one year (Fig. 5b); and results with error terms greater than this should be rounded outwards to five years; those that calibrate between cal AD 1000 and 12,277 cal BC (14,226 cal BP) should be rounded outwards to 10 years (or five years when error terms are less than ±25 BP) (Fig. 5c); those that calibrate between this date and 20,050 cal BC (25,000 cal BP) should be rounded outwards to 10 years (Fig. 5d); and those that calibrate between this date and the limit of calibration should be rounded outwards to 20 years (Fig. 5e). Ages that calibrate across these boundaries should be rounded to the larger value. Determinations that are calibrated using mixed-source or marine calibration should be round outwards to 10 years, or to 20 years for Pleistocene samples (Fig. 5f).

So, for example, using this protocol the date ranges of GrA-24663 calculated using the probability method (Fig. 4a–b) become: 750–680 cal BC (11% probability) or 670–630 cal BC (5% probability) or 570–380 cal BC (79% probability). Sometimes ranges can merge on rounding.

Single-point summary statistics, such as the mean, the median, or an intercept point estimate, are poor approximations of the calibrated date and should not be used (Telford et al. 2004).

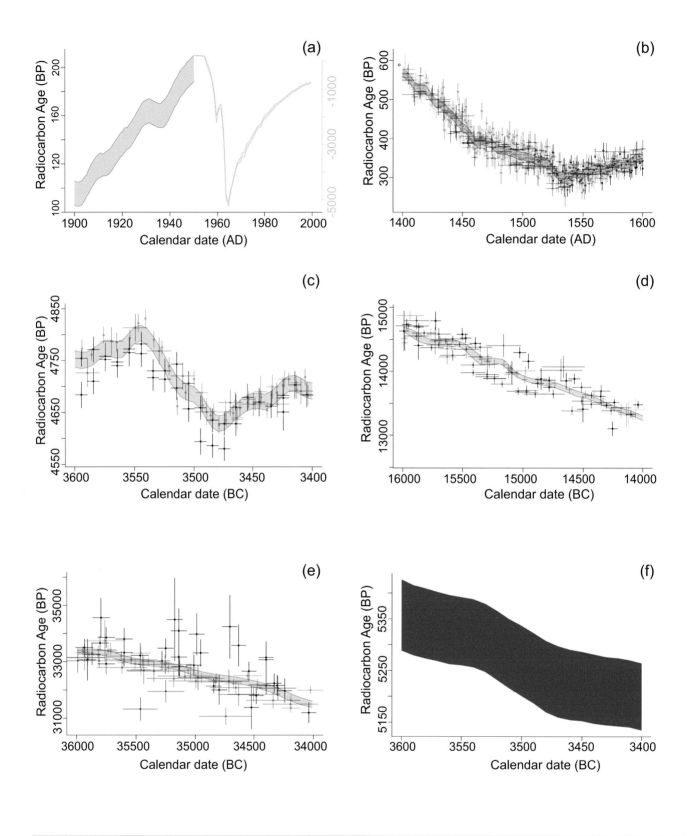

Figure 5 Example sections of the currently agreed calibration curves relevant for England, showing their varying resolution (image by P. Marshall):

(a) IntCal20 (AD 1800–1950) and NH1 (1950–2000) calibration curves (Reimer et al. 2020; Hua et al. 2021);

(b) IntCal20 (AD 1400–1600) calibration curve (Reimer et al. 2020) and data points (http://intcal.qub.ac.uk/intcal13/);

(c) IntCal20 (3400–3600 BC) calibration curve (Reimer et al. 2020) and data points (http://intcal.qub.ac.uk/intcal13/);

(d) IntCal20 (14000–15000 BC) calibration curve (Reimer et al. 2020) and data points (http://intcal.qub.ac.uk/intcal13/);

(e) IntCal20 (34000–35000 BC) calibration curve (Reimer et al. 2020) and data points (http://intcal.qub.ac.uk/intcal13/);

(f) Marine20 (3400–3600 BC) calibration curve (Heaton et al. 2020).

1.6 Reservoir effects

Reservoir effects occur when the carbon that is incorporated into a sample during life is not in equilibrium with the contemporary atmosphere. This gives the sample an apparent radiocarbon age older than that of a contemporary terrestrial sample. In order to obtain an accurate calibrated date for such a sample, it is necessary to correct the apparent age during the calibration process using the relevant reservoir offset.

Most samples requiring reservoir correction derive from the marine environment. On average, the apparent age of a marine sample is about 400 radiocarbon years older than the contemporary atmosphere. This offset is caused by the time it takes atmospheric radiocarbon to exchange into ocean bicarbonate, and by the dilution effect caused by the mixing of surface waters with upwelling ^{14}C-depleted deep water. Consequently, the marine reservoir correction deviates locally from the global average.

Marine samples should be calibrated using the internationally agreed marine calibration curve (Marine20; Heaton et al. 2020) and an appropriate local ΔR ('Delta R') correction. These values have been measured either on marine samples that were collected at a known date before AD 1950 in a known location, or on **perfect pairs** of contemporary terrestrial and marine samples. A database of such values is available at http://calib.org/marine/, although data from around the English coast are sparse. It should be noted that ΔR values need to be recalculated for use with Marine20, as methodological advances mean that those calculated for use with IntCal13 are no longer appropriate. **Marine reservoir effects** can vary, not only spatially, but also temporally, and this is an area of active research. Calibration of samples from marine mammals, which can range widely and incorporate carbon from a wide variety of reservoirs, is complex.

Hard-water error, or the **freshwater-reservoir effect**, is local and extremely variable. It can be of considerable magnitude. This arises from the dilution of dissolved atmospheric carbon in the water with ^{14}C-free geological carbonate from the surrounding bedrock. If it is necessary to date samples that come from organisms that live fully submerged in freshwater (such as certain species of ostracod or pondweed), then a local correction must be available or measured — either on local freshwater material collected at a known date before AD 1950 or on **perfect pairs** of contemporary terrestrial and fully freshwater samples. There is presently no central repository of freshwater offset values for England, and so existing data must be sought in the literature on a case-by-case basis.

Estuarine conditions are produced by the mixing of freshwater and marine waters. Reservoir effects within estuaries are thus again extremely variable and, if it is necessary to date samples that obtained their carbon from the waters of the estuary, then, again, a local correction must be applied. If this is not already available, it must be measured as part of the study.

It should be noted that in many cases it is possible to avoid offsets deriving from hard-water or estuarine conditions by dating emergent plants (such as *Cladium mariscus*), which fix their carbon by photosynthesis from the atmosphere and thus, in calibration terms, count as fully terrestrial. In cases where the origin of the dated material is unclear (for example, organic sediments), the presence of a reservoir offset is potentially indicated by a δ^{13}C value that is enriched in comparison to equivalent material of a terrestrial origin (*see* §1.4).

Dietary offsets can occur in samples of bone, as the food consumed by an organism can derive from a variety of sources that potentially can have marine and freshwater, as well as terrestrial, reservoirs. Bone **collagen** derives mainly from the protein component of the diet, and bone **apatite** mainly from the whole diet. For accurate calibration, the proportion of the diet of a sampled individual deriving from each source must be estimated and the radiocarbon reservoir of each dietary source determined. Appropriate calibration data can then be mixed proportionately.

So, for example, a radiocarbon age on bone collagen from a human whose protein intake consisted of 80±10% terrestrial herbivore and 20±5% marine fish would be calibrated using 80±10% IntCa20 and 20±15% Marine20 (with an appropriate local ΔR correction). As marine, freshwater and estuarine reservoirs are always depleted in radiocarbon in comparison to the contemporary atmosphere, a mixed-source

Figure 6: A 'perfect pair': humans and cow burial (photograph by Wessex Archaeology, Creative Commons License).

sample that is calibrated erroneously using a fully atmospheric calibration curve will always be too old (*see* §5.2).

In England dietary offsets in human bone are generally modest in scale, although these can be significant for producing accurate, high-precision chronologies. Larger offsets do sometime occur in Viking and later individuals, but are by no means universal. A component of marine or freshwater foods in the diet can generally be inferred from stable isotopic evidence. Marine foods lead to enriched $\delta^{13}C$ and $\delta^{15}N$ values, whereas freshwater foods generally lead to enriched $\delta^{15}N$ values only. Stable isotopic measurements relevant to dietary reconstruction should therefore be undertaken routinely when dating human bone. Estimating the absolute contributions of different dietary sources in an individual is extremely complex, and specialist advice should be sought in cases where it is required.

Comparing dates on human skeletons and contemporary terrestrial material is a way to check directly for the presence of a dietary offset (Fig. 6). A male human skeleton from Eriswell, Suffolk provided a radiocarbon age of 1640±20 BP (UB-6347), and the horse skeleton in the same grave provided a statistically consistent radiocarbon age of 1611±20 BP (UB-6348; T'=1.1; T'(5%)=3.8; df=1). This indicates that there was no significant offset in the radiocarbon age of the human bone in this individual. Dating of such **perfect pairs** should be undertaken where the opportunity arises, especially where a wider programme of radiocarbon dating of human bone is being undertaken on a site.

In English archaeology, there are generally suitable samples of terrestrial material available, which should be preferred for dating, as they avoid the complexities and additional uncertainties outlined in this section. Occasionally, however, the best material for dating could derive from a non-terrestrial source, in which case specialist advice should be sought.

Key facts: calibration and reservoir effects

Calibration is an essential step that converts a radiocarbon age to the calendar timescale. It only needs to be undertaken separately where Bayesian Chronological Modelling is not employed, as it forms part of the modelling process. Each measurement (or weighted mean) must be calibrated using a calibration curve appropriate to the reservoir from which the sample derived its carbon.

In the northern hemisphere the internationally agreed calibration curves for samples that date before AD 1950 are currently:

- ■ terrestrial samples: (IntCal20; Reimer et al. 2020)

- ■ marine samples: (Marine20; Heaton et al. 2020), with an appropriate ΔR correction (http://calib.qub.ac.uk/marine/)

- ■ freshwater samples: (IntCal20; Reimer et al. 2020), with appropriate local offset (calculated as part of the study or gleaned from the literature)

- ■ bone from omnivores or carbonised food residues on pottery where the proportions of different reservoirs have been estimated: **mixed-source calibration** (individual mixture of the above)

When publishing calibrated dates, the calibration curve and method used should be specified. Laboratory codes should always be given, along with the radiocarbon age and experimental uncertainty (error) for legacy data that are not published elsewhere in the study.

1.7 Citation of radiocarbon dates

Protocols for reporting newly commissioned radiocarbon dates and chronological models are described below (§3.6).

It is often necessary, however, to cite radiocarbon dates obtained by previous workers in discussion. These results should be re-calibrated using the same method and calibration curve as used in the rest of the study, and the laboratory number, radiocarbon age and uncertainty estimate provided. For example, in the form: '… the transition from marine to freshwater peat accumulation had certainly occurred by 4680–4340 cal BC (HAR-1831; 5650±70 BP; Jordan et al. 1994, 165) at nearby Ashcott Heath'. If not provided elsewhere in the publication, references should also be given to the curve and method used for calibration and, if appropriate, details of any reservoir correction applied.

2 Bayesian Chronological Modelling

For a single sample, **calibration** of the radiocarbon age (or of the **weighted mean** if there is more than one determination on the sample) is sufficient to convert the radiocarbon measurement to the calendar timescale (*see* §1.5). There is a limit to the precision that can be achieved this way, as a measurement on a cereal grain — actually harvested on one day of one particular year — typically produces a calibrated date range that spans more than a century. But the **probability** distribution (and range) of the calibrated date does estimate that point in time accurately to within the quoted uncertainty, and that date does provide a **range-finder** for the date of the deposits or objects sampled.

However, when we have a group of radiocarbon ages from samples that are in some way related, then more sophisticated statistical approaches are required.

2.1 The need for statistical analysis

Statistical analysis of groups of radiocarbon dates is needed because the simple calibration process makes a statistical assumption: that the date of the sample is equally likely to fall at any point on the calibration curve used. For a single measurement, this assumption is usually valid. But as soon as there is a group of measurements that are related in some way (e.g. that are from the same site), then this assumption is violated. For example, if the first sample from a site is of Bronze Age date, then the chances are that the samples subsequently dated will also be Bronze Age.

The effect of ignoring this issue is illustrated in Figure 7, which shows a series of calibrated radiocarbon dates (on well-associated, short-lived samples, *see* §3.2.2 and §3.2.3) for two sites. When faced with interpreting a graph such as Figure 7, most archaeologists inspect the probability distributions, visually assessing their widest limits (perhaps excluding low parts of the probability distributions from the edges of the graph), and estimate that activity on Site A happened between *c.* 2025 cal BC and *c.* 1750 cal BC; that this activity took place over several hundred years; and that Site B was occupied at a similar time and for a similar period.

These interpretations are importantly wrong. The calibrated dates in Figure 7 have been simulated, using a process of 'back calibration' from samples of known calendar date. For example, if we have a sample that actually dates to 1932 BC and produces a measurement with an error term of ±30 BP, then we can transfer the calendar date through the calibration curve to the radiocarbon age scale. Each simulation will produce a slightly different value because of the error term on the radiocarbon age. For example, 1932 BC might produce a simulated radiocarbon age of 3612±30 BP. This is then calibrated to produce a realistic estimate of the calibrated radiocarbon date that would be produced by a sample of this calendar age, in this case 2120–2090 cal BC (3% probability) or 2040–1880 cal BC (92% probability; using the probability method). So for the data in Figure 7, because we have simulated the radiocarbon dates ourselves from known calendar ages, we know that Site A was in use for 200 years between 2000 BC and 1800 BC and that Site B was in use for 40 years between 1925 BC and 1885 BC. In both cases, without formal statistical analysis, there is a very

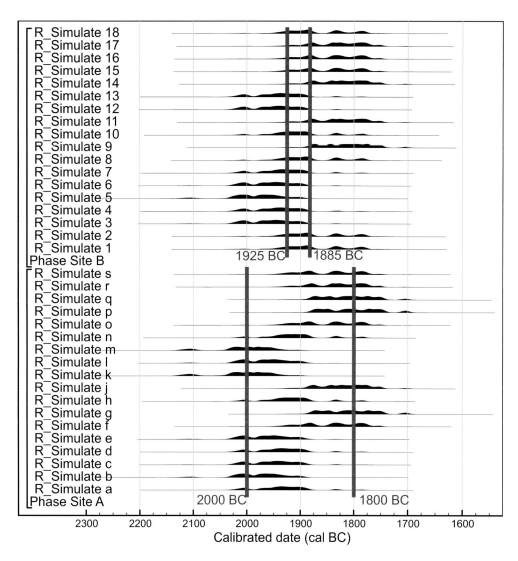

Figure 7: Calibrated radiocarbon dates (Stuiver and Reimer 1993; Reimer et al. 2020) from two fictitious early Bronze Age sites (A and B). The radiocarbon ages have been simulated from samples that actually date every 25 years between 2000 and 1800 BC (site A) and every five years between 1925 and 1885 BC (site B) (image by A. Bayliss).

significant risk that past activity will be interpreted as starting earlier, ending later and enduring for longer than was actually the case.

Since estimating radiocarbon ages is a probabilistic process, calibrated radiocarbon dates scatter around the actual calendar dates of the samples. Given the uncertainties on most calibrated radiocarbon dates and the relative brevity of much human activity, this statistical scatter on the dates can be substantial in comparison to the actual duration and dates of the archaeological activity in question. Proportionately, the quantity of scatter is greater when the actual period of dated activity is short and/or the number of radiocarbon dates is large (compare, for example, the scatter on the

calibrated radiocarbon dates outside the actual calendar dates of the samples in Figure 7, Site A with those in Figure 7, Site B).

2.2 Bayesian Chronological Modelling

Bayesian statistics provide an explicit, probabilistic method for combining different sorts of evidence to estimate the dates of events that happened in the past and for quantifying the uncertainties of these estimates. This enables us to account for the relationships between samples during the calibration process.

The basic idea is encapsulated in **Bayes' theorem** (Fig. 8), which simply states that we analyse the new data we have collected about a problem ('the standardised likelihoods') in the context of our existing experience and knowledge about that

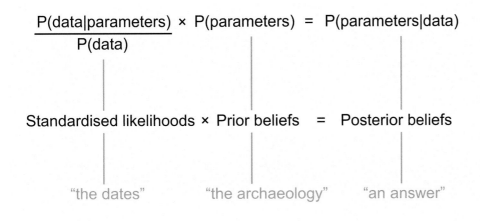

$$\frac{\text{P(data|parameters)}}{\text{P(data)}} \times \text{P(parameters)} = \text{P(parameters|data)}$$

Standardised likelihoods × Prior beliefs = Posterior beliefs

"the dates"   "the archaeology"   "an answer"

Figure 8: Bayes' theorem (image by A. Bayliss).

---

problem (our **'prior beliefs'**). This enables us to arrive at a new understanding (our **'posterior belief'**), which incorporates both our existing knowledge and our new data. This is not the end of the matter, however, since today's posterior belief becomes tomorrow's prior belief, informing the collection of new data and their interpretation as the cycle repeats.

Lindley (1991) provides an accessible introduction to the principles of Bayesian statistics.

2.2.1 Components of a Bayesian chronological model

When constructing a Bayesian chronological model, the scientific dates form the **'standardised likelihoods'** component of the model (Fig. 8). They are the data to be reinterpreted in the light of archaeological prior beliefs. Most often these are calibrated radiocarbon dates, but it is also possible to include dates from coins, historical sources, dendrochronology and the results of other scientific dating methods such as luminescence and archaeomagnetic dating.

The second component in a chronological model is composed of our **'prior beliefs'**. These are no more than a formal, mathematical expression of our understanding of the archaeological context of the problem that we are modelling.

Sometimes it is clear that we have strong archaeological evidence of the relative chronology of the samples that have been dated: for example, when one dated grave cuts another. This type of clear relative sequence provided by archaeological stratigraphy often provides strong constraints on the calibration of dates from related samples in a site sequence (*see* §5.7). The tree-ring series used during wiggle-matching (*see* §5.6) also provide strong prior beliefs for the relative dating of the sampled rings. At a wider scale, dates can be combined with other forms of archaeological information that provide relative sequences, such as typology (e.g. Needham et al. 1998) or seriation (e.g. Bayliss et al. 2013).

Sometimes this seems so obvious that its importance in chronological modelling is not at first apparent. The most common information of this kind is that a group of radiocarbon dates are related. Most often this is because the samples collected relate to a single site, although other forms of relatedness, such as samples associated with particular pottery styles, can also be used (e.g. Healy 2012). To return to the example considered in Figure 7, if we model the radiocarbon dates from each site using only the information that each group of measurements derives from a site, which began at some point in time and then was used relatively continuously until it ended, then we get the models shown in Figure 9. These statistical models are clearly able to distinguish between the scatter of radiocarbon dates that derives from the actual duration of activity in the past, from scatter that simply arises from the probabilistic process of radiocarbon dating. The models both provide formal date estimates for the start and end of the relevant sites that are compatible with the actual dates input into the simulation, and are clearly able to distinguish that the activity at Site B was of much shorter duration than Site A.

Figure 9 also illustrates that Bayesian Chronological Modelling is not simply about refining the calibration of radiocarbon dates, although the outputs of the model (shown in black) are clearly more precise than the simple calibrated radiocarbon dates (shown in outline). It is also possible to calculate distributions for the dates of events that have not been dated directly

by radiocarbon measurements, such as the date when a site was established or abandoned. For example, the parameter *'start A'* (Fig. 9) has been calculated using all the radiocarbon dates from the site (a–s) and the interpretation that it was occupied continuously until it was abandoned. All of these measurements have also been used to estimate the date when the site went out of use (*'end A'*; Fig. 9). By comparing estimates such as these, it is possible to calculate new probability distributions to estimate the duration of phases of activity (e.g. *'use A'*; Fig. 10).

The posterior beliefs that are output by a Bayesian model are known as **posterior density estimates** (the distributions in black in Figure 9). These

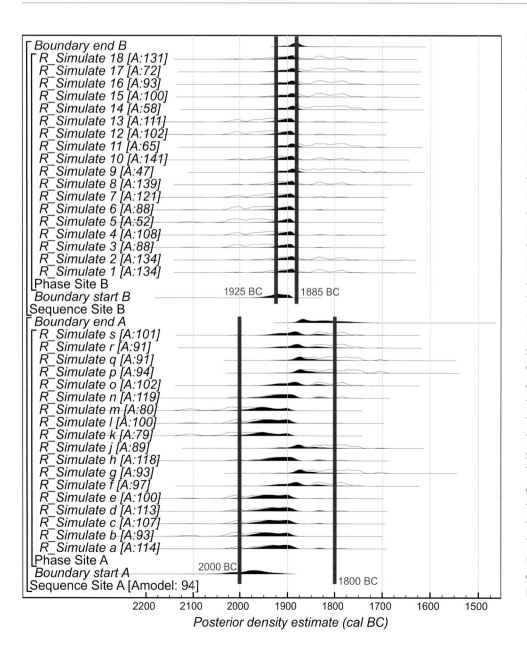

Figure 9: Probability distributions of the same simulated dates from the two fictitious early Bronze Age sites shown in Figure 7. Each distribution represents the relative probability that an event occurs at a particular time. For each of the dates two distributions have been plotted: one in outline, which is the result of simple radiocarbon calibration; and a solid one, based on the chronological model used. Model and individual indices of agreement are shown in square brackets. Other distributions correspond to aspects of the model. For example, the distribution *'start A'* is the estimated date when site A was established. The large square brackets down the left-hand side of the diagram, along with the OxCal keywords, define the overall model exactly (http://c14.arch.ox.ac.uk/oxcal.html) (image by A. Bayliss).

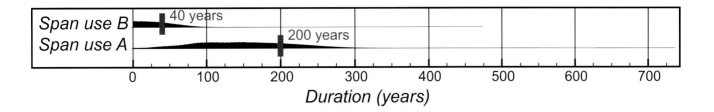

Figure 10: Probability distributions showing the number of calendar years during which Site A and Site B were occupied, derived from the model shown in Figure 9 (image by A. Bayliss)

probability distributions can be summarised as ranges, which are known as **Highest Posterior Density intervals** and are expressed in italics to distinguish them clearly from date estimates that have not been produced by modelling.

2.2.2 Model calculation, validation and comparison

In theory, once the model has been defined, the posterior beliefs can be calculated using Bayes' theorem (Fig. 8). In practice, however, almost all chronological models have so many independent parameters that the number of possible outcomes to consider at a useful resolution makes such a calculation impractical (the exception is wiggle-matching, *see* §5.6). For this reason, **Markov Chain Monte Carlo (MCMC) methods** are used to provide a possible solution set of all of the parameters of the model. The degree to which a truly representative solution set has been generated is called **'convergence'**. A variety of diagnostic tools have been proposed to validate convergence, and all the software packages that have been developed to undertake Bayesian Chronological Modelling employ some form of convergence checking (that employed in OxCal is described by Bronk Ramsey 1995, 429).

Stability of the model outputs is not the only criterion by which models can be validated. We also need to consider whether the two components input into the model, the 'prior beliefs' and the 'standardised likelihoods', are compatible. This compatibility can be at a particular level, for example considering whether a sample really fits into the sequence at the position where it has been placed in the model, or at a general level, for example, examining whether phase 1 is really earlier than phase 2.

At present the validation of Bayesian models is an inexact science, although several statistical approaches have been developed to assist in the identification of incorrect models and incompatible prior beliefs and standardised likelihoods. Statistics alone cannot be relied upon to identify all the incorrect components of a model, and so archaeological critique of the character and context of the dated material, and scientific understanding of the complexities of radiocarbon dating, are key elements in model validation (*see* §3.2.2 and §3.2.3).

The first statistical method for assessing the compatibility of the components of a model is formal statistical **outlier analysis** (Christen 1994). In this method each measurement is given a prior probability of being an **outlier** (typically a low probability like 5%) and the date is further down-weighted in the model if it is inconsistent with the rest of the available information. The output from the model is affected by this down-weighting, and in addition to the normal model outputs, a posterior probability for the sample being an outlier is also generated. Either this probability can be used to identify outliers and remove them, or the model that incorporates outlier weighting can be accepted (technically, this approach is a form of model averaging; Bronk Ramsey et al. 2010; *see* §5.7). This approach is available in several of the software packages that have been developed to undertake chronological modelling.

Secondly, we can consider the **agreement indices** provided by the OxCal software (Bronk Ramsey 1995, 429; 2009a, 356–7). These are not derived from a formal statistical approach and have the disadvantage that there is no theoretically defined cut-off applicable in all cases, but they do have the advantage that the model itself is not affected by the calculations. They are also easy to calculate and have proved useful and robust in practice for a wide range of case studies.

The individual index of agreement provides a measure of how well the posterior distribution (i.e. that incorporating the prior beliefs and shown in black in Figure 9) agrees with the standardised likelihood (i.e. the calibrated date shown in outline in Figure 9); if the posterior distribution is situated in a high-probability region of the standardised likelihood, then the index of agreement is high; if it falls in a low-probability region, it is low. Most individual indices of agreement in a model should be above 60 (a threshold value obtained by simulation). Usually those that fall below this level are statistical outliers (see, for example, '9' in Figure 9), although a very low index of agreement can also suggest that part of the model is wrong and needs further examination.

An overall index of agreement is then calculated for the model from the individual agreement indices, providing a measure of the consistency between the prior information and the scientific dates. Again, the model index of agreement generally has a threshold value of 60, and models that produce values lower than this should be subject to critical re-examination (for example, phase 1 is possibly not actually earlier than phase 2). It should be noted that what is important statistically is that a model fails to meet the threshold (Amodel: 60), and so alarm bells are triggered. A higher model index of agreement is not necessarily 'better', because the agreement index is also influenced by the strength of the constraints incorporated into a model, so a model with more informative prior information will — all other things being equal — have a lower index of agreement than one with less informative prior beliefs.

While in practice outlier analysis and agreement indices almost always identify the same dates or prior constraints as problematic, these two approaches are alternatives and should not be used in the same model. They are, however, both compatible with rigorous archaeological critique of the character and context of the dated material and meticulous scientific examination of the complexities of radiocarbon dating. These are critical constituents in model validation and should be employed whichever statistical approach is chosen.

Having identified problems with particular dates, or with particular components of a model, these need to be resolved. Sometimes this involves a reassessment of the overall structure of a model — was phase 1 really earlier than phase 2, or could they have overlapped? In other cases, single dates need to be reinterpreted individually and handled appropriately. The best way of dealing with such dates depends on our assessment of why they are problematic. The most common categories are:

- **Misfits** – dates that do not fit in the expected stratigraphic position, or that are inaccurate for some technical reason. Generally, samples that prove to be residual can be used as *termini post quem* for their contexts, but intrusive samples or inaccurate dates need to be excluded from the analysis. Sometimes it is possible to reinterpret the stratigraphy.

- **Outliers** — the 1 in 20 dates whose true calendar date lies outside the 2σ range. These must be retained in the model, as their exclusion would statistically bias the results; outlier analysis can be useful.

- **Offsets** — measurements that are systematically offset from the calibration data by a knowable amount. **Reservoir effects** can be accounted for in the calibration process (*see* §1.6), if necessary, **old-wood** offsets can be accounted for in the modelling process (Dee and Bronk Ramsey 2014); other types of offset will be rarely, if ever, encountered in English archaeology.

Having constructed a plausible chronological model, the next step in Bayesian modelling is to assess its sensitivity to different aspects of the model being incorrect. This construction of alternative models is called **sensitivity analysis**. One component of a model is changed, and it is rerun. The **posterior density estimates** from the original model and its variant are then compared. When these outputs are very similar, the model can be regarded as insensitive to the component of the model that has been varied. When the outputs differ markedly, the model is sensitive to that component. Sensitivity analyses are useful not only in determining how far the outputs of a model are stable, but also help us to identify which components of a model are most critical.

This introduction to Bayesian Chronological Modelling inevitably masks many of the technical complexities of the method. It aims to provide enough understanding of the principles employed to enable archaeologists to collaborate actively with their specialist modellers. It cannot be emphasised enough that modelling is a collaborative exercise that relies essentially on the skills, experience and understanding of participating archaeologists. The explicit expression of relevant archaeological knowledge and its appropriate inclusion in models is as critical a step in the modelling process as is the selection and dating of samples.

A general introduction to the application of the Bayesian approach to archaeological data is provided by Buck et al. (1996). More specific introductions to building Bayesian chronologies in archaeology are provided by Bayliss et al. (2007a) and Bayliss (2007).

Key facts: Bayesian Chronological Modelling

Statistical methods are required to handle relationships between dated samples. **Bayesian statistics** enable calibrated radiocarbon dates to be combined with other information we might have about a chronological problem, producing **posterior beliefs** that take account of all the evidence. **Prior beliefs** can be simply that all the dated samples are from a single site or associated with the same kind of pottery, but could include relative sequences provided by stratigraphy, seriation or the growth-rings in wood or charcoal.

Most Bayesian Chronological Models are calculated using **Markov Chain Monte Carlo (MCMC) methods**. The stability of a model is assessed by its **convergence**, and the compatibility of components of the model using **outlier analysis** or **agreement indices**. Most dates that are incompatible with a model are **misfits**, **outliers** or **offsets**. The best way to incorporate such samples in a model depends on an assessment of why they are problematic. The stability of model outputs to variations in the prior information included or the modelling approach adopted is assessed by constructing a series of alternative models as part of a **sensitivity analysis**.

3 The Bayesian process

The use of **Bayesian statistics** for the interpretation of radiocarbon dates reinforces the need for clear problem definition, the requirement for rigour in sample selection, and the need for explicit consideration of our pre-understandings in interpretation. Attention to these issues is, however, essential in any programme of scientific dating. Consequently, the iterative approach to sample selection and chronological modelling that has been crafted out of repeated practice over the past twenty-five years is applicable whether or not Bayesian statistics are ultimately used for the interpretation of the data (Fig. 11). This process enables best value to be obtained from any programme of radiocarbon dating.

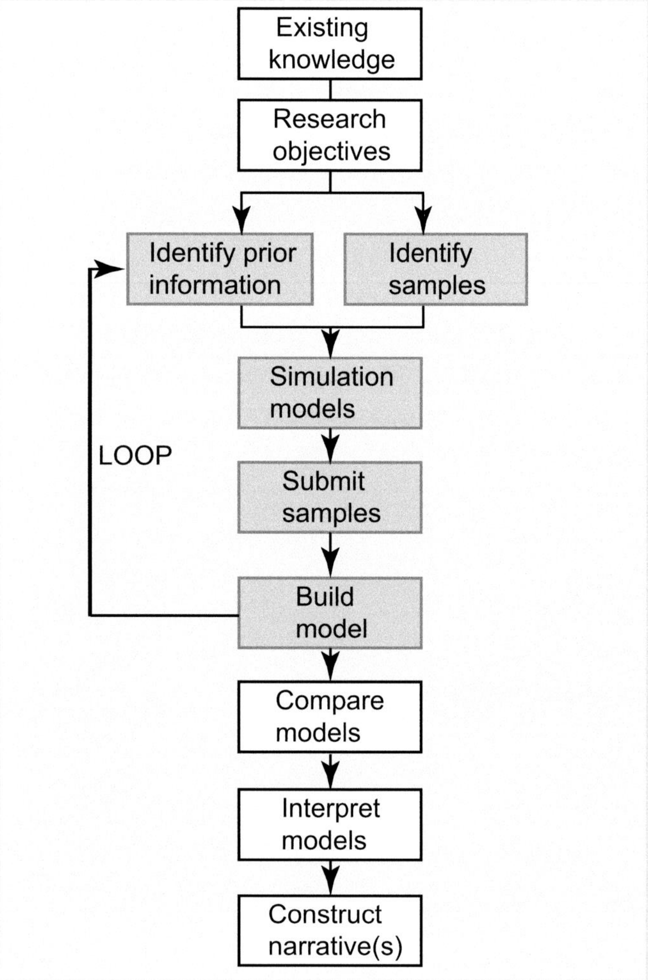

3.1 Problem definition

The first step in the process is to consider the range of potential archaeological questions that a dating programme could address (Fig. 11). These are, of course, framed within the context of existing knowledge (often summarised in regional or period resource assessments).

Key is the need to identify why dating for the artefact, activity or site is required. This factor will determine the precision of dating needed to resolve the question of interest. Secondly, we must consider whether the question can be resolved at the level of the study being undertaken, or whether we wish to submit samples that will ultimately contribute to wider objectives, such as those identified in regional and period research frameworks.

For example, consider a site of undiagnostic form, lacking any material culture. We think that it could be prehistoric or early medieval, but need to determine to which period the site belongs. Dating to within a few centuries will resolve this issue.

Or, perhaps we have excavated part of an enclosure, and revealed enough of the plan and sufficient associated material culture to be confident we have a Neolithic causewayed enclosure. A recent synthesis has determined that this type of monument was constructed over a period of approximately 150 years between the late 38th and

Figure 11: The Bayesian process (image by A. Bayliss).

23

late 36th centuries cal BC (Whittle et al. 2011, figs 14.11–14.12). So, obtaining a few radiocarbon dates that, when calibrated, will place the monument in the mid-fourth millennium cal BC will not tell us anything that we do not already know. We need a full programme of radiocarbon dating and chronological modelling to produce a chronology that is precise to about half a century, so that we can place our site in the emerging narrative for the appearance and use of this monument type in southern Britain (ibid, figs 14.16 etc).

Or, perhaps we have excavated a pit containing a highly decorated Beaker vessel, accompanied by a large concentration of carbonised plant remains and some articulated animal bone. Nationally, we may wish to trace the direction of the spread of Beakers across Britain. Regionally, we may wish to know when Beakers first appeared in our region.

Obtaining high-quality radiocarbon dates (*see* §3.2.2 and §3.2.3) for one assemblage on our site will tell us its date of deposition to within a century or two, and could place the pottery in the earlier or later part of the national currency of Beaker pottery. But, once several assemblages have been dated from our region, time transgressive patterns at a much higher resolution will become apparent (cf Jay et al. 2019, fig. 2.1).

3.2 Identifying a pool of suitable samples

Once we have defined the objectives of our proposed dating programme, the next step is to identify a pool of samples that is potentially suitable for dating (Fig. 11).

Table 2: Guide to optimal sample size for material commonly dated by AMS (for further information you **must** contact your chosen laboratory, as both preferred and, in particular, minimum sample sizes do vary considerably by facility).

Material	Optimal sample size (before pre-treatment)	Comment
Wood (not waterlogged or charred)	60mg	Single tree-ring from increment borer usually sufficient.
Bone & antler	2g	Cortical bone (e.g. a long bone) is best.
Calcined bone	4g	Single fragment of pure white bone is best.
Residues on pottery — pitch, charred food	50mg	1cm^2 of visible residue is usually adequate.
Charred plant remains & charcoal	60mg	A single charred cereal grain is usually adequate (*c.* 10mg).
Waterlogged wood	5g	1cm^3 is usually adequate.
Waterlogged plant remains	200mg–5g	The size needed is very variable as it depends on water content; a large macrofossil such as an alder cone is usually viable.
Organic sediment	3g	1cm^3 is usually datable – **but beware** (*see* §3.2.3)!
Other materials	Contact your radiocarbon dating laboratory before submitting samples of other materials.	

3.2.1 Retrieving and storing samples

First, of course, it is necessary to retrieve those samples during fieldwork and to store them until they are needed for radiocarbon dating (*see* §4.1).

With the advent of AMS, the concept of a radiocarbon sample fundamentally changed. The required sample size is now so small (Table 2) that it is physically possible to obtain a radiocarbon measurement on almost any organic material that is recovered during fieldwork. Consequently, all

material should be collected, packaged and stored in a way that does not compromise its potential for radiocarbon dating.

Dry wood
Samples of wood that is not carbonised or waterlogged are usually obtained from standing buildings, either as offcuts when parts of timbers are replaced during repair works or as cores removed by an increment borer during dendrochronology (*see* English Heritage 1998, §2.2.4; Fig. 12). Samples should be clearly labelled, and the presence of the heartwood/

Figure 12: Removal of a core sample for tree-ring dating (© Historic England Archive).

sapwood boundary, sapwood and waney edge/ bark recorded. They should be stored in cardboard boxes or plastic bags. Samples intended for radiocarbon wiggle-matching should not be glued to wooden laths or marked-up with ink for tree-ring measurement. Any evidence of past timber treatment should be recorded, and details of the chemicals used obtained if possible.

Bone and antler

Generally, samples of bone and antler may be washed in water, marked using Indian ink or otherwise clearly labelled, dried and stored in plastic bags or cardboard boxes (Baker and Worley 2019, 23–4). Reconstruction of breaks using glue should be avoided. Samples intended for dating should not be chemically consolidated. Specialist advice should be obtained during the fieldwork stage of a project if consolidation is essential, so a sub-sampling strategy can be devised to retain sufficient unconsolidated material for dating. Fragile specimens may be wrapped in aluminium foil. Especial care should be taken in

recording and recovery of articulating animal bone groups (Baker and Worley 2019, 18), which are likely to be preferred for dating (see §3.2.2).

Calcined bone

Calcined bone may also be washed in water and stored in plastic bags. Fragile bone should be protected from further fragmentation by storage in acetate boxes.

Surface and absorbed residues from pottery sherds

A variety of surface residues on pottery sherds can be dated by AMS, including carbonised food crusts (Fig. 13), sooting and decoration and repairs undertaken in pitch. Absorbed fatty acids from ceramics can also been dated. Sherds displaying visible residues, or intended for absorbed lipid analysis, should not be washed. All these residues can be contaminated by the plasticizers used in plastic bags, bubble-wrap and the lids of some types of glass vial. Such sherds should be air-dried, wrapped in aluminium foil, clearly labelled and then stored in acetate boxes or plastic bags.

Figure 13: Carbonised residue adhering to a ceramic sherd (photograph by P. Marshall).

Especial care should be taken of groups of refitting sherds with ancient breaks, which are likely to be preferred for dating (*see* §3.2.2).

Carbonised plant remains (including charcoal)

Carbonised plant remains, including charcoal, are generally recovered by water flotation from bulk sediment samples that have been taken according to an explicit sampling strategy (*see* Campbell et al. 2011, §3). Carbonised material should be air-dried, clearly labelled and stored in glass vials, acetate boxes or plastic bags. If the material is stored in plastic bags, care should be taken to ensure that it is not crushed during storage.

Waterlogged wood

Waterlogged wood is sometimes recovered either during excavation, or during sampling for other waterlogged plant remains or organic sediment. Samples of structural timber fall into two categories: large timbers with ring sequences that have failed to produce dendrochronological dating, which require wiggle-matching (*see* §5.6); and short-lived pieces of wood. Sampling for the first category of material should be as set out for dendrochronology (English Heritage 1998, §2.2.5; Brunning and Watson 2010, §3.6.5). For the second category, ideally six pieces of short-lived material from different elements of an archaeological structure that can be dated should be retained (e.g. wattle panel). All samples should be kept wet in a plastic bag (or wrapped in plastic), clearly labelled using waterproof pen on waterproof labels in another plastic bag, and then wrapped in a third plastic bag. They should then be kept in a cold store or fridge until wood identification, dendrochronology and radiocarbon dating can be undertaken (Brunning and Watson 2010, §3.8). Biocides must not be used.

Waterlogged plant remains

Waterlogged plant remains can be recovered by wet sieving of bulk sediment samples that have been taken according to an explicit sampling strategy (*see* Campbell et al. 2011, §3), but they can also be retrieved from samples of organic sediment that have been taken from exposed sections or by coring. Once isolated they should be clearly labelled, stored in a small amount of

water in a glass vial or plastic tube and kept in a cold store or fridge until needed for dating. Samples should *not* be stored in Industrial Methylated Spirits (IMS) or alcohol.

Organic sediment

Samples from vertical sections of sediment can be taken either by hand excavation, using monolith tins, or by coring (Historic England 2015a; Fig. 14). Care must be taken to ensure that a continuous sequence of sediment is retrieved and that it is not contaminated during recovery. It is beneficial to take an overlapping series of monolith tins or cores so that samples from undisturbed positions throughout a sequence can be obtained taken. If possible, a closed-chamber corer (such as a 'Russian' or 'Livingstone' corer) should be used to take two adjacent cores (no more than 0.2m apart) overlapping by half the length of the core-sections. 'Gouge' augers, typically with an open semi-cylindrical chamber, should not be used. However, in situations where this is unavoidable, extreme care should be taken to minimise the possibility of contamination. Similarly, when cores are taken by power augers, the holes are not sleeved and therefore contamination can be an issue. The outer surface of core samples, which is most likely to have become contaminated during extraction, should be cleaned before packaging and storage. All samples should be located three dimensionally in relation to the local datum points e.g. Ordnance Survey grid (OSGB36; UK onshore) or UTM (WGS84) using appropriate surveying equipment (*see* Historic England 2015b).

Most organic sediments of Holocene date recovered from England are sufficiently well preserved that datable waterlogged plant macrofossils will be recovered from a 10mm thick slice of sediment obtained from a section, monolith tin or corer. Some sediments, however, are humified to the point that plant macrofossils do not survive. In these circumstances, radiocarbon dating of bulk sediment has to be considered (*see* §3.2.3).

The materials described above constitute over 95% of the radiocarbon samples dated from England, although a wide range of other archaeological finds can be dated. These include:

Figure 14: Coring to obtain a geoarchaeological sequence through deposits (photograph by Alice Dowsett, ©Archaeology South-East).

marine and freshwater shell, both of which require reservoir corrections (*see* §1.6); skin, leather and parchment; hair, wool and horn; insect chitin; ivory; paper; and vegetable resin used as mastic for hafting stone tools. It is also possible to date the carbon included in the steel component of some ferrous objects, and carbon dioxide fixed from the atmosphere by lime mortar as it sets. Not all laboratories date all these material types, and if you are interested in dating any of them you should obtain specialist advice before submitting samples.

This section considers samples obtained during new fieldwork. Some projects can require dating of materials that have been stored in archaeological and museum archives for many decades (Fig. 15). Such objects may have been chemically conserved, and may have been neither collected nor stored in ideal conditions. This does not necessarily mean that they cannot be successfully dated, but specialist advice in such circumstances is essential.

Figure 15: Archaeological material stored in an empty cigarette packet (photograph by K. Nichols, ©Wessex Archaeology).

3.2.2 Archaeological criteria for identifying suitable samples

Once the organic material from the project has been retrieved and catalogued, the next step is to identify samples that are potentially suitable for dating (Fig. 11). This is a complex task that requires both rigorous understanding of some challenging archaeological issues (discussed in this section), and consideration of the wide range of scientific complexities that beset radiocarbon dating (*see* §3.2.3).

The association between the datable material and the archaeological activity that is of interest is paramount (Waterbolk 1971). This relationship, between the dated event (e.g. the shedding of an antler) and the target event (e.g. the digging of a Neolithic ditch with that antler), is never known but is inferred from archaeological evidence (such as wear or burning on the antler). The basis of this inference, and its security, must be specifically considered for every potential sample.

The most secure association is when the datable material comes from an object that is of intrinsic interest. In this case, it would not matter if the sample was unstratified. An example is a carbonised food crust adhering to a diagnostic pottery sherd, if the objective of the dating programme is to obtain a chronology for that ceramic type.

Such cases are, however, comparatively rare. It is usually the context of the sample that is of interest: the date of the ditch, or of the site or of the associated material culture. This is even more important if you have a stratigraphic sequence of deposits that you wish to use as prior information in a Bayesian chronological model. Stratigraphy, of course, provides evidence about the relative sequence of contexts. Radiocarbon

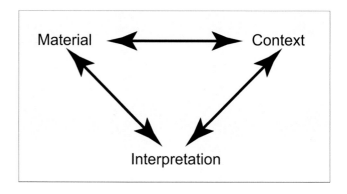

Figure 16: The relationship between interpretation, an archaeological context and the material recovered from it (image by A. Bayliss).

29

dating does not date contexts, it dates samples. So, the calibrated radiocarbon dates can only be constrained using the stratigraphic sequence of contexts if the dated samples were freshly deposited in the contexts from which they were recovered. This is where interpretation of the taphonomy of the datable material comes into play (Fig. 16).

There is no such thing as a perfect sample for radiocarbon dating. All potential samples have their strengths and weaknesses, and a key part of sample selection is to assess the risk of submitting an item for dating. The crucial archaeological interpretation is to establish whether a potential sample is likely to have been residual (or, less frequently, intrusive) in the context from which it was recovered. This can be inferred with varying degrees of confidence.

Archaeological association

There are many types of evidence that can be considered in assessing sample taphonomy, most of which rely on the results of other archaeological analyses and assessments (faunal, geoarchaeological, environmental, etc.). The availability of the wide range of information that is necessary for the selection of samples for radiocarbon dating is a major constraint in timetabling dating in the overall project programme (see §4.6).

In most studies, dating a sample is a means to date a context. In such cases, the vast majority of samples submitted for radiocarbon dating from England can be included in the following taphonomic categories, which are listed in roughly descending order of reliability:

a) Bones found in articulation and recorded in the ground as such (Fig. 17a). These samples would have been still connected by soft tissue when buried and hence from people or animals that were not long dead.

b) Articulating bones identified as such during specialist analysis (Fig. 17b). These samples could have been articulated in the ground (but not recognised as such) or have only been slightly disturbed before burial. The presence of more

than one bone from the same individual provides evidence that such samples are close in age to their contexts. The security of this inference increases as the number of articulating bones increases. Occasionally both bones are not present, but the condition of the articular facet suggests that the articulating bone was present in the ground.

c) Bones with refitting unfused epiphyses identified during specialist analysis (Fig. 17c; *see* b, above).

d) Food residues from groups of refitting pottery sherds or from a group of sherds from a single vessel (Fig. 17d). Carbonised residues on the interior of the vessel probably represent charred food (rather than sooting). As the sherds refit or much of a pot survives, the vessel has a good chance of being in the place where it was originally discarded.

e) Calcined bone from distinct individuals (human or animal) and carbonised plant remains from cremation deposits (Fig. 17e).

f) Wood used in the construction of archaeological structures (e.g. waterlogged hurdles, charred posts, timbers from standing buildings; Fig. 17f).

g) Carbonised plant remains functionally related to the context from which they were recovered (e.g. charcoal from a hearth or kiln; Fig. 17g).

h) Antler tools discarded on the base of ditches and other negative features (Fig. 17h), thought to be functionally related to the digging of the features (e.g. in a flint mine). This inference is most secure when the tine is embedded in the base of the cut, but could be based on use-wear such as battering on the posterior side of the beam/burr/coronet.

i) Waterlogged plant remains from archaeological contexts (e.g. a well). These are probably in the place where they were originally deposited, or they would not have remained waterlogged and survived (Fig. 17i).

j) Single fragments of short-lived carbonised plant material from coherent, often friable or ashy, dumps of charred material: inferred on the basis of their coherence and fragility to be primary disposal events (e.g. 'placed' deposits in pits; Fig. 17j).

k) Paired bones (usually from different sides, e.g. left and right ulnae) thought to be from a single individual on the basis of size, morphology, etc.; Fig. 17k; *see* c, above) but less secure.

l) Grave goods, which must have been in circulation at the time of burial but may have had a history of use before deposition (Fig. 17l).

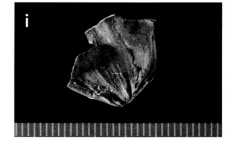

Figure 17 (a): articulating horse skeleton (photograph by Wessex Archaeology, Creative Commons License);

(b) re-articulating cattle distal tibia and astragalus (photograph by P. Marshall);

(c) juvenile cattle 1st phalanx diaphysis, with refitting unfused proximal epiphysis (photograph by P. Marshall);

(d) refitting sherds with internal carbonised residue — the small area deliminated by the white line is a guide to the size of sample required (photograph by A. Bayliss);

(e) two fragments of calcined bone (photograph by P. Marshall);

(f) a pit containing a timber structure (© Worcester Archaeology);

(g) a kiln (photograph by P. Weston, © Archaeological Services WYAS);

(h) antler picks found at the base of an excavated ditch (photograph by Wessex Archaeology, Creative Commons License);

(i) sweet chestnut pericarps (© Historic England Archive).

m) Disarticulated human bones from burial monuments, which are probably functionally related with the site, even if they do not necessarily represent primary deposition (Fig. 17m).

n) Material from 'occupation' spreads: samples that can be related to human activity (e.g. cut-marked bone, calcined animal bone) can be more secure than those that might derive from previous natural events (e.g. charcoal) (Fig. 17n).

o) Food residues from single pottery sherds: *see* d, above) but less secure (Fig. 17o). The inference that the sherd is not residual is based on the fragility of the pottery concerned.

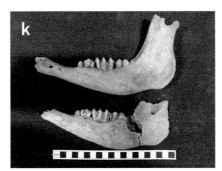

(j) burnt mound pit (© Worcester Archaeology);

(k) a pair of cattle mandibles thought to derive from the same animal (photograph by P. Marshall);

(l) sampling the Prittlewell drinking horn (photograph A. Bayliss).

(m) mass human grave deposit (photograph by Wessex Archaeology, Creative Commons License);

(n) midden deposit containing animal bone and other refuse (© Historic England Archive);

(o) carbonised residue adhering to the interior of a single sherd (photograph by P. Marshall);

(p) excavated post holes and beam slots of a prehistoric building

(photograph by Wessex Archaeology, Creative Commons License);

(q) cattle skull at the base of a ditch (© Dorset Museum).

p) Material derived from the postholes of timber buildings; on the basis of experimental archaeology (Reynolds 1995), putatively derived from the occupation of the structure (Fig. 17p).

q) Well-preserved disarticulated animal bones: submitted on the basis that the latest date from a group of measurements should provide a *terminus post quem* that is (hopefully) not too much earlier than the actual date of interest (e.g. multiple dates from basal fills of field boundaries) (Fig. 17q).

This list is not comprehensive, but it does give an indication of the range of issues that should be considered when assessing the relationship between the target event and the dated event of potential radiocarbon samples. Other material that has a high chance of being residual, such as disarticulated bones from the upper fills of features, or low densities of charred plant material that has been retrieved by processing large environmental samples, is rarely suitable for dating.

The golden rule is that every potential sample should be considered residual unless there is a plausible argument showing that it was freshly deposited in the context from which it was recovered.

Taphonomy of organic sediments

So far, we have considered only those samples that derive from archaeological excavations. Many projects, however, are concerned with samples of bulk organic sediment from sequences used for environmental reconstructions. The **taphonomy** of the material within these samples can be complex. The question we have to ask is the same, however: is the carbon that will be dated from the sediment *in situ*, and is it directly related to the past event of interest?

Several fractions may be dated from bulk sediment:

- Identifiable waterlogged plant macrofossils; thought to be from plants that grew on or around the sampled site as the sediment accumulated.

- 'Fulvic acid' fraction of bulk sediment: this is the acid soluble fraction and is often too recent. It is no longer dated routinely, although measurement on this fraction can be found in the literature or undertaken for experimental reasons.

- 'Humic acid' fraction of bulk sediment: this is the acid insoluble, alkali soluble fraction. It is thought to derive from the decay of plant material that grew on the site as the sediment accumulated.

- 'Humin' fraction of bulk sediment: this is the acid and alkali insoluble fraction. It is thought to consist of the physical remains of the plant material that grew on the site.

- 'Total organic' fraction of bulk sediment: this is the solid fraction that remains after the acid soluble fraction (Fulvic acid) has been removed. It consists of the 'humic acid' and 'humin' fractions combined.

- Bulk samples of microfossils (e.g. foraminifera, pollen).

There are risks inherent in dating any of these materials. The likelihood that the datable remains in the sediment grew *in situ* on the wetland surface, or were incorporated from plants growing on the contemporary landsurface, must be assessed by careful consideration of their context. What is the lithology and geomorphology of the site? Are the sediments horizontally bedded? Is the wetland an ombrotrophic mire, or a minerotrophic fen or marsh? If the wetland is fed by run-off, then what else could have washed in? Are there exposed coal measures or peat deposits, for example, farther upstream? If there are plant macrofossils in the profile, what species are present? What are their characteristics? Do they have invasive roots (e.g. *Phragmites* sp.)? If so, are we sure that the isolated material is not root, or has not been pushed down into earlier sediments from above? What is the organic content of the sediment? What is its pH?

Once more, there are no perfect samples. The object of this deliberation is to select for dating the fraction or material from within a sediment which most accurately reflects the age of its deposition (*see* §3.2.3).

Single-entity dating

The imperfection of almost all potential radiocarbon samples brings us to the need for single-entity dating (Ashmore 1999). This is a strategy that minimises the risk that the submitted sample will contain residual or reworked material, by dating material that certainly derives from a single organism (e.g. a single cereal grain).

We can examine this strategy using simple statistics. Consider, for example, a deposit where 1 in 10 of the recovered short-life charred plant remains are residual. Imagine, perhaps, that we have excavated a malting kiln containing charred barley from its final firing. Most of the barley grains will have come from that firing, but a small proportion could derive from previous firings or the clay fabric of the collapsed kiln itself and thus be earlier. If we date a single grain from this deposit, the radiocarbon date will have a 90 percent chance of dating to the time when the context was formed and a 10 percent chance of being earlier. If we obtain two radiocarbon dates from this deposit, each from a single grain, then there will be a 99 percent chance that at least one of the two dates will relate to the time when the deposit was formed. If, however, we bulk those two grains together and obtain one radiocarbon date, then there will be a 19 percent chance that at least one of those grains is residual and so the radiocarbon date is earlier than the time when the deposit was formed. The greater the number of items that are bulked together, the lower the probability that the sample will contain only freshly deposited material. If 10 seeds were to be bulked together for dating from this deposit, then there would be a chance of less than 1 in 3 that the resultant radiocarbon date would accurately date the formation of the context. Obviously, the scale of the offset will depend on the actual proportion of residual material in a sample and its date in relation to the time when the deposit from which it was recovered was formed.

Not all bulk samples necessarily contain residual material. For example, the dating of multiple single fragments of short-life charcoal from a fired feature, such as a hearth, will often give results that are statistically consistent both with each other and with a measurement on a bulk sample of short-lived material from the same context, although this is not always the case (cf Tintagel Castle, Bayliss and Harry 1997). With the routine availability and increasing precision of AMS, however, the submission of bulk samples where they can be avoided is an unnecessary risk.

There are still, however, a few situations where it could be necessary to submit bulk materials.

- Food residues from ceramic sherds probably derive from meals that contained several ingredients, and so, by definition, such residues are not single-entities. Carbonised residues probably relate to the last use of the vessel, but lipids can accumulate during the time when the vessel was used.

- Waterlogged plant macrofossils and bulk sediment are not so unproblematic. Much of the weight of waterlogged material (sometimes 80%) is water, and so to obtain enough carbon for dating even by AMS it is often necessary to bulk together several plant macrofossils (e.g. seeds of the same species).

- Carbonised plant remains that are too small for single-entity dating (e.g. cereal glume bases).

- Microfossils (such as foraminifera, pollen and most species of ostracod) again have to be bulked to provide enough carbon for dating even by AMS.

- Fractions of bulk sediment, by definition, derive from multiple sources.

Figure 18 is a flow diagram that provides a step-by-step guide to assessing the archaeological suitability of potential samples for radiocarbon dating.

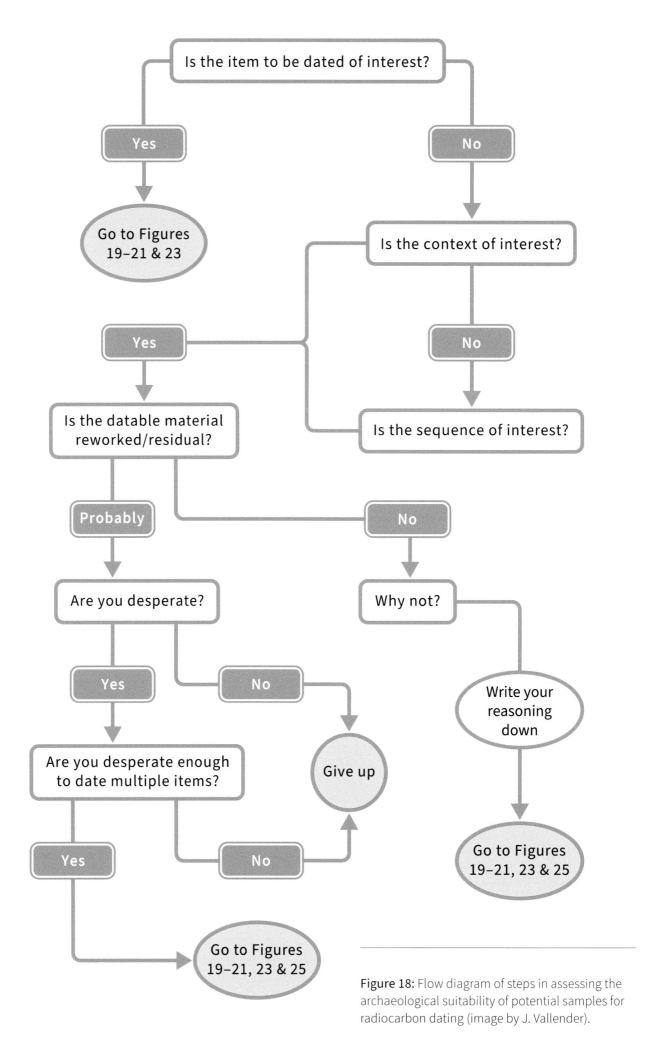

Figure 18: Flow diagram of steps in assessing the archaeological suitability of potential samples for radiocarbon dating (image by J. Vallender).

3.2.3 Scientific criteria for identifying suitable samples

In the previous section, we have considered the first basic criterion that a sample must meet before it is considered suitable for dating: that it must be securely associated with the archaeological activity that is of interest. There are two other criteria that a potential sample must meet, however, before it can be considered for dating. These are considered in this section.

First, the carbon in the sampled organism must be in equilibrium with the carbon in the atmosphere (or some other well-characterised reservoir) at the time when the organism died.

Old-wood effect

By far the most common source of error of this type is the **old-wood effect**, where dates are obtained on wood or charcoal from a long-lived tree. The carbon in a tree-ring dates from the year in which that tree-ring was laid down, and so the carbon from the centre of a 300-year-old oak tree will be 300 years old while that tree is still growing — this is why wood dated by **dendrochronology** can be used to construct a **radiocarbon calibration curve**.

For this reason, all samples of wood and charcoal should consist of:

- material from a known position in a tree-ring series (such as rings sampled for **wiggle-matching**),

- twigs or the outer rings of the tree (a single years' growth is optimal, but the number of growth rings to bark should be recorded if a single growth-ring cannot be isolated),

- if twigs are not available, samples have to be taken from short-lived species (e.g. *Corylus avellana*) or branch-wood, although in this case a wood-offset of a few decades cannot be ruled out, and sophisticated mathematical approaches will be required to utilise the resulting measurement (*see* §2.2.2).

All samples of wood or charcoal must be aged and identified to the highest taxonomic level possible by a suitable specialist before submission for dating.

Figure 19 is a flow diagram that provides a step-by-step guide to assessing the scientific suitability for radiocarbon dating of carbonised plant material that has passed the steps illustrated in Figure 18; and Figure 20 provides a similar flow diagram for assessing the suitability of waterlogged plant material.

Other age-at-death offsets

Sooting on pottery sherds usually derives from the fuel used on domestic hearths during cooking. If this was wood derived from relatively short-lived material (e.g. branches collected from hedgerows), then there is unlikely to be a significant offset. If the fuel used was constructional timber from a recently-demolished building or from peat, then more substantial offsets are more likely. Unfortunately, the fuel used on the fire that left a soot deposit on a sherd is rarely known, and so the scale of any potential offset is also unknown. It is for this reason that internal carbonised residues on pottery sherds (which likely derived from carbonised food) are generally preferred for radiocarbon dating, although, of course, external residues that have been chemically characterised as food crusts are also suitable. Decoration or repairs on pottery vessels in pitch, which is derived from wood resin, provide dates that are in equilibrium with the contemporary atmosphere; but decorations or repairs in bitumen or coal-tar, which are petroleum-derived, do not.

Calcined bone can also exhibit an age-at-death offset derived from the incorporation of carbon from the pyre fuel during the cremation process (Snoeck et al. 2014). The scale of offsets of this kind is currently uncertain, as is their prevalence in the past. Most pairs of measurements on calcined bone and on short-lived charcoal from the same cremation deposit undertaken so far seem to be statistically consistent (Lanting et al. 2001), and so significant age-at-death offsets in prehistoric cremation deposits seem uncommon in practice (but *see* Olsen et al. 2012).

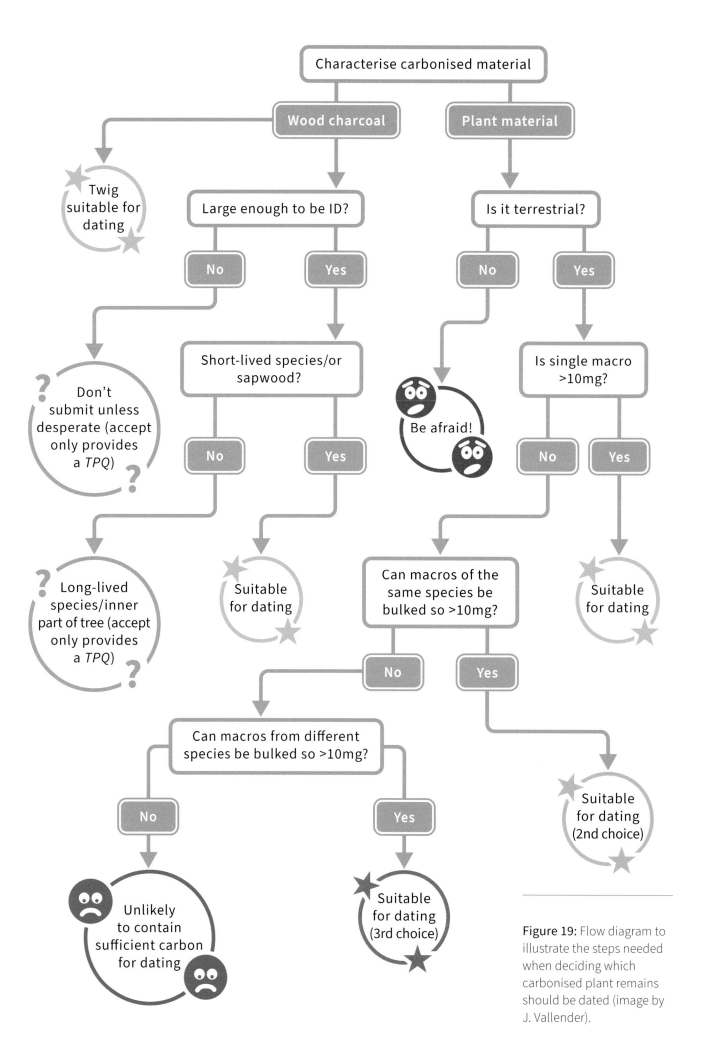

Figure 19: Flow diagram to illustrate the steps needed when deciding which carbonised plant remains should be dated (image by J. Vallender).

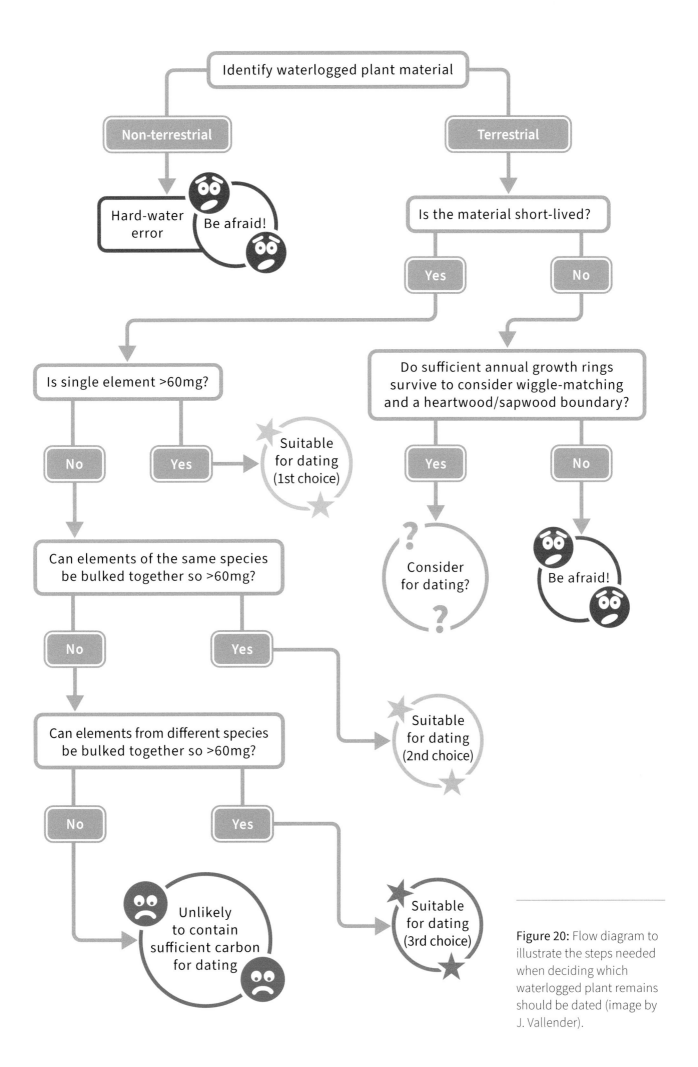

Figure 20: Flow diagram to illustrate the steps needed when deciding which waterlogged plant remains should be dated (image by J. Vallender).

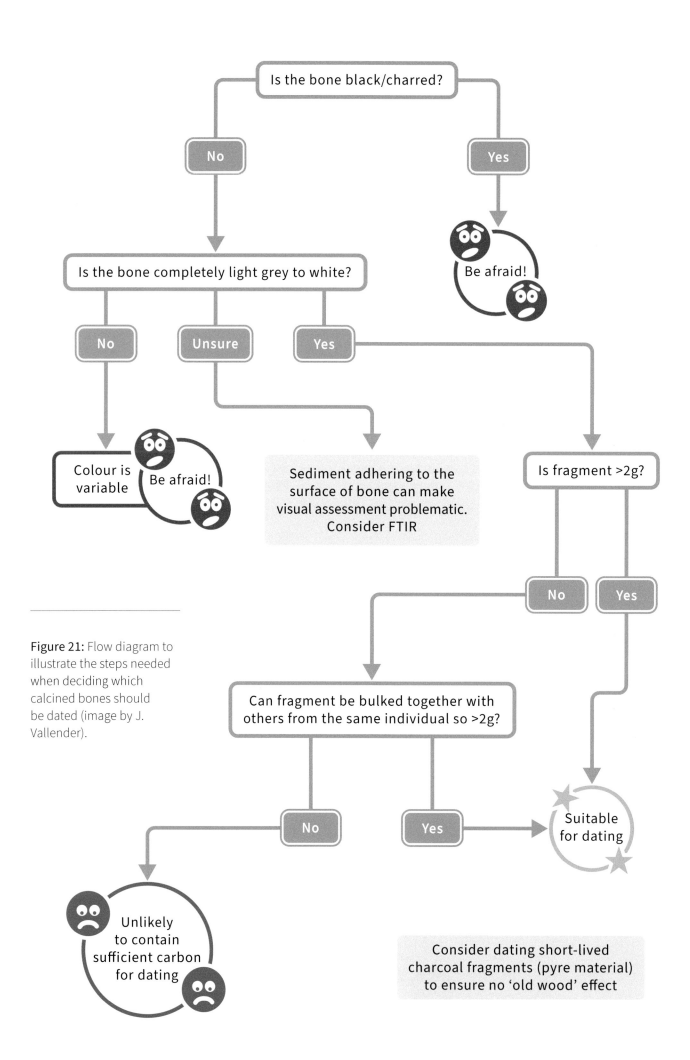

Figure 21: Flow diagram to illustrate the steps needed when deciding which calcined bones should be dated (image by J. Vallender).

Figure 21 is a flow diagram that provides a step-by-step guide to assessing the scientific suitability for radiocarbon dating of calcined bone samples that have passed the steps illustrated in Figure 18.

Age-at-death offsets can affect bone from older individuals of species that live for some decades. The offset arises from the time it takes carbon from the diet to be incorporated into bone collagen. As individuals become older, the average difference between the radiocarbon age of the carbon in the bone collagen and the carbon in the contemporary atmosphere becomes greater, particularly in men (Hedges et al. 2007). Given life-expectancy in the past, bone turnover **offsets** are unlikely to be of practical relevance except for the most high-precision applications.

Other effects that can complicate the relationship between the carbon absorbed by the sampled organism in life and the contemporary atmosphere are isotopic fractionation, which should be dealt with by age-calculation (*see* §1.4), and reservoir effects (*see* §1.6).

Reservoir effects
As described above, the best policy for dealing with samples that exhibit reservoir effects is avoidance. This means that animal bones should be identified before dating to ensure that they come from a terrestrial mammal. In England, there will almost always be suitable material of fully-terrestrial origin, which can be dated in preference to a sample from a non-terrestrial reservoir. In those cases, where it seems likely that such samples are the best material available, specialist advice should be sought.

Some information is available about the **marine reservoir** of English coastal waters, and so samples of local marine origin, such as shellfish and some foraminifera can be dated, and the

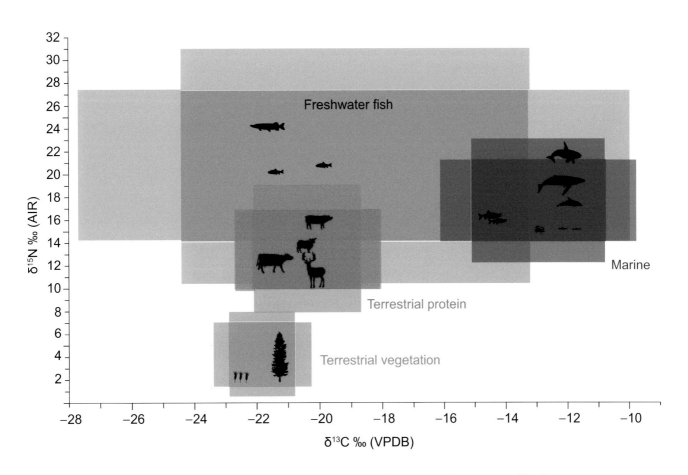

Figure 22: Simplified summary of stable carbon and nitrogen values for terrestrial, marine and freshwater ecosystems. Error boxes (light shading) are derived from standard deviation on isotopes for food-types (adapted from Beavan and Mays 2013).

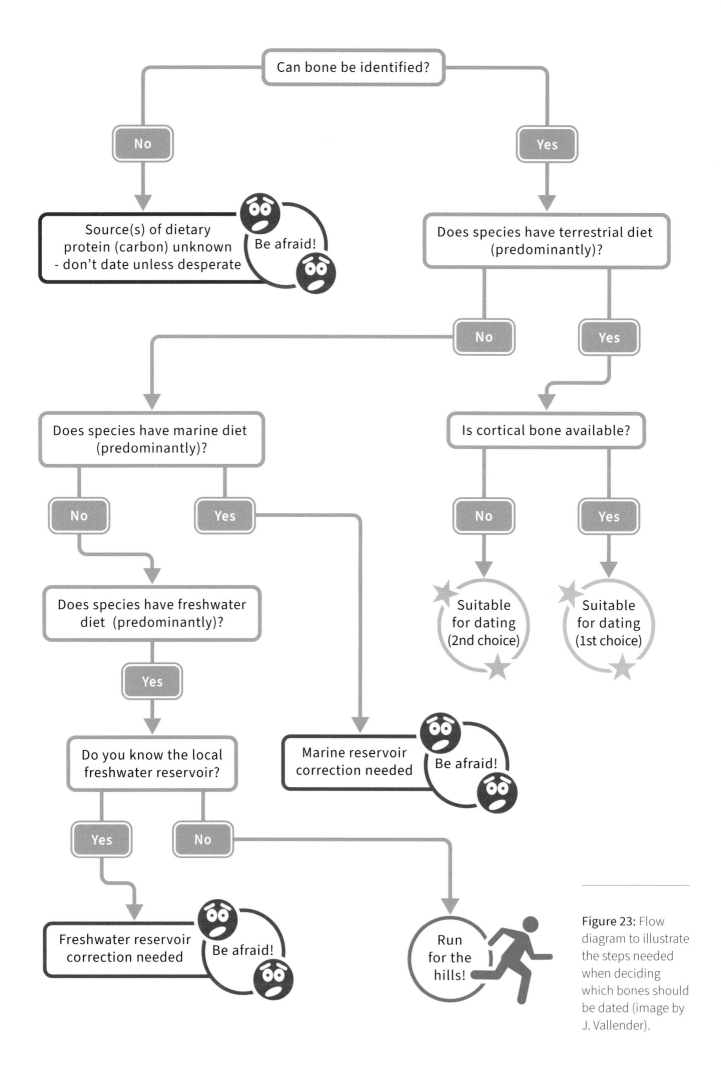

Figure 23: Flow diagram to illustrate the steps needed when deciding which bones should be dated (image by J. Vallender).

resultant measurements calibrated using the internationally agreed marine calibration curve (Marine20) and an appropriate local ΔR correction (*see* §1.6). The error on the ΔR correction compounds that on the radiocarbon measurement on the sample itself, so the resultant calibrated date is less precise than would be the case with a measurement on a contemporary terrestrial sample. Other samples of marine origin can be more problematic. Most fishing appears to have been in-shore until *c*. AD 1000 and trading in preserved fish, as far as is known, of modest scale. Consequently, usually it will be valid to calibrate results on fish bone using a local marine correction. It is sometimes difficult to know which ΔR correction is appropriate, however, from later fish remains, which could come from deep-water fisheries or from traded salt-fish. Similarly, marine mammals can range widely, and it is again difficult to know which ΔR correction is appropriate. Food residues from pottery sherds can also potentially derive from marine sources.

In contrast, little is known about reservoir effects in freshwater and estuarine conditions in England. So, if materials from these reservoirs are selected for dating, it is necessary to measure the local reservoir offset as part of the study. Specialist advice should be sought in these circumstances. **Hard-water offsets** can occur, not just in freshwater fish and shells, but also in food residues from pottery sherds. The most common type of material encountered where freshwater reservoirs can be an issue are waterlogged plant macrofossils from submerged plants, for example *Potamogeton*. Animals that rely on freshwater resources, such as beaver or waterfowl, can also exhibit a **freshwater reservoir effect** offset. Again, avoidance is the best policy, and material from fully-terrestrial or emergent plants or from terrestrial animals should be isolated and dated wherever possible. **Hard-water offsets** can also occur in results on bulk fractions of organic sediments, where the sediments were made up of submerged plants. In this case, the potential presence of an offset can be indicated by an enriched $\delta^{13}C$ value.

Correcting for **dietary offsets** in bone samples is also difficult, largely because of uncertainties in estimating the proportions of different food sources in past diets accurately from stable isotopic values (Fig. 22). This has been done most convincingly where non-terrestrial dietary components are large, or where there is a restricted range of food sources (e.g. Arneborg et al. 1999). Modest offsets from small (<10%) components of non-terrestrial foods are very difficult to identify and quantify accurately. **Dietary offsets** in bone **apatite** derive from whole diet, and so potentially are much lower than those from bone **collagen**, which derives mainly from the protein component of diet.

In England, significant dietary offsets are rare in human bone before the medieval period, and even then are by no means universal. The presence of a marine component in the diet can be indicated by enriched $\delta^{13}C$ and $\delta^{15}N$ values, and enriched $\delta^{15}N$ values can indicate the presence of a freshwater fish component (although the interpretation of these values is particularly complicated, and there can be other explanations of such values). If elevated $\delta^{13}C$ and $\delta^{15}N$ values (above *c*. −18.0‰ and +12.0‰) are encountered when dating human bone, specialist advice should be sought.

Figure 23 is a flow diagram that provides a step-by-step guide to assessing the scientific suitability for radiocarbon dating of animal and human bone that has passed the steps illustrated in Figure 18.

Natural contamination

The second scientific criterion a sample must meet if it is to be considered suitable for radiocarbon dating is that it must not be contaminated by any other carbon-containing material. This is impossible in practice, as the climate of England is damp and so, at the very least, the organic component of groundwater will have added contaminants to the sample. The principal contaminants are dissolved carbonates from bedrock, and fulvic and humic acids, which arise from the decay of organic matter in soils. This is why the pretreatment of almost all samples begins with an acid step (*see* §1.2) to remove dissolved carbonates (which are of geological age) and **fulvic acids** (which are usually more recent as they are often mobile in groundwater).

Humic acids are generally less mobile in groundwater than fulvic acids and, as they arise from the decay of organic matter, are frequently of the same age as the sample to be dated. This is often the case, for example, with fragile carbonised plant remains that are only given 'an acid wash' in the laboratory. In this case both the carbonised material and the humic acid complexes within it that remain after the acid step are dated. Humic acids are, however, soluble in alkali and can be mobile on alkaline geologies where anomalously young ages can occur (e.g. OxA-11663 from Silbury Hill, Wiltshire; Marshall et al. 2013, table 4.1).

Targeting material for dating from organic sediments

The potential mobility of humic acids is thus a material consideration in choosing the best material to date from organic sediments. This is a complex issue, and there is no single best solution. The choice of material to date from a sediment is affected by its preservation, geology and hydrology.

The material of choice is a single-entity waterlogged terrestrial plant macrofossil (e.g. an alder cone). This is based on the principle that dates on terrestrial plant macrofossils are generally more reliable than those on 'bulk' samples of the sediment matrix, as the source of carbon in the former is known and, in a single macrofossil at least, is not made up of heterogenous material that could be of different ages (Walker et al. 2001). Waterlogged plant macrofossils are generally fragile and do not usually survive reworking, but they are not entirely unproblematic. It is both possible for earlier material to be in-washed and for later material to be pushed down from above. This can be investigated by dating more than one sample from a key horizon (see §3.3.2 below).

Phragmites australis — as a marginal aquatic plant where the majority of its growth above ground occurs in air rather than in water, and with rhizomes that are readily recognisable — is often chosen as suitable single entity for radiocarbon dating. However, the rhizomes are far-creeping and the roots often reach to considerable depth,

so a *Phragmites* sp. culm base or rhizome can be considerably younger than the sediment in which it occurs. For this reason, it is preferable to choose horizontally bedded leaves and/or stems, even if they cannot be precisely identified, as there is a better chance they will be the same age as the deposit in which they are found. Alternatively, taxa such as *Schoenoplectus* spp. and *Cladium mariscus* can be used as these have shallower roots and short creeping rhizomes. Caution should also be exercised when using seeds that are dispersed by water. These can travel some distance before being deposited and thus can be reworked. Twigs are generally more robust, and can also survive reworking.

Most radiocarbon laboratories, however, require at least 60mg of waterlogged plant material for dating, and so most waterlogged macrofossils recovered from sediment are too small for dating on their own. When no macrofossils large enough for single-entity dating are found in a sediment, or where these are so atypical that there must be a concern that they are exogenous to the sediment, a number of macrosfossils can be bulked together for dating. This introduces the risks of bulk samples (see §3.2.2), but again the source of the carbon dated is known. Experience has shown that bulking together a large number of macrofossils of the same kind (e.g. birch seeds) can be better than bulking together the remains of heterogenous species, as it is more likely that the latter will include intrusive/reworked material.

Strenuous efforts must be made to isolate macrofossils before the dating of bulk sediment is considered (c. 80% of organic sediments of Holocene date from England **do** contain macrofossils). If identifiable plant macrofossils do not exist within the sediment, it is advisable to sample elsewhere. If macrofossils are still not preserved, then it will be difficult and expensive to obtain a reliable chronology for the sequence. In these circumstances the importance of the information contained in the deposits must be considered. Will the resources, probably considerable, necessary to provide an accurate chronology for the sediment sequence be justified by the importance of the environmental/geoarchaeological record?

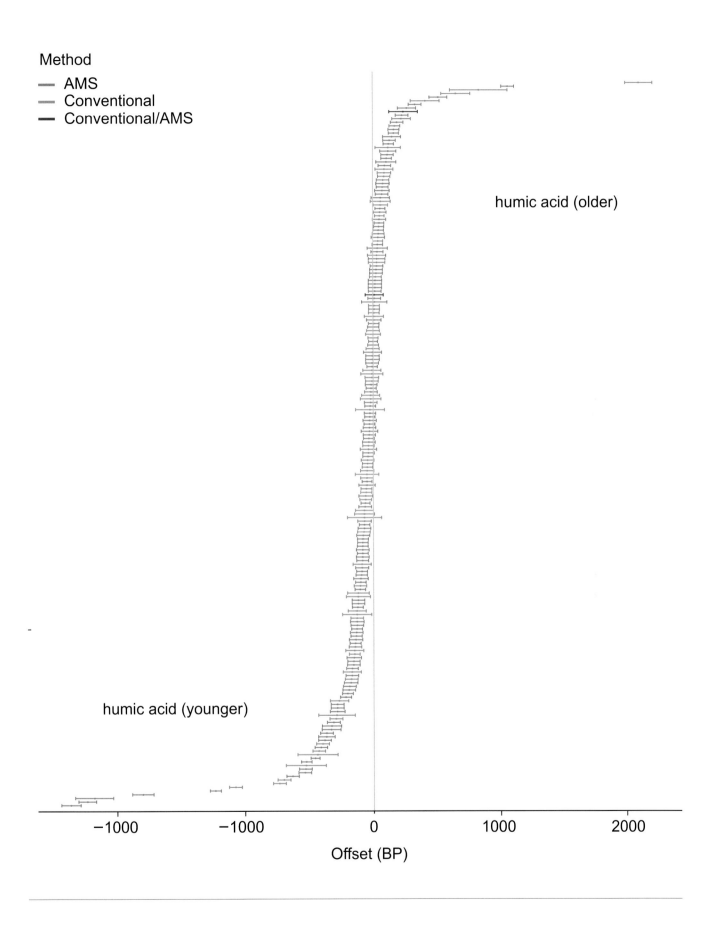

Figure 24: Offsets between replicate radiocarbon measurements on the humic acid and humin fractions of bulk sediment of Holocene age (error bars are at 1σ) (image by P. Marshall).

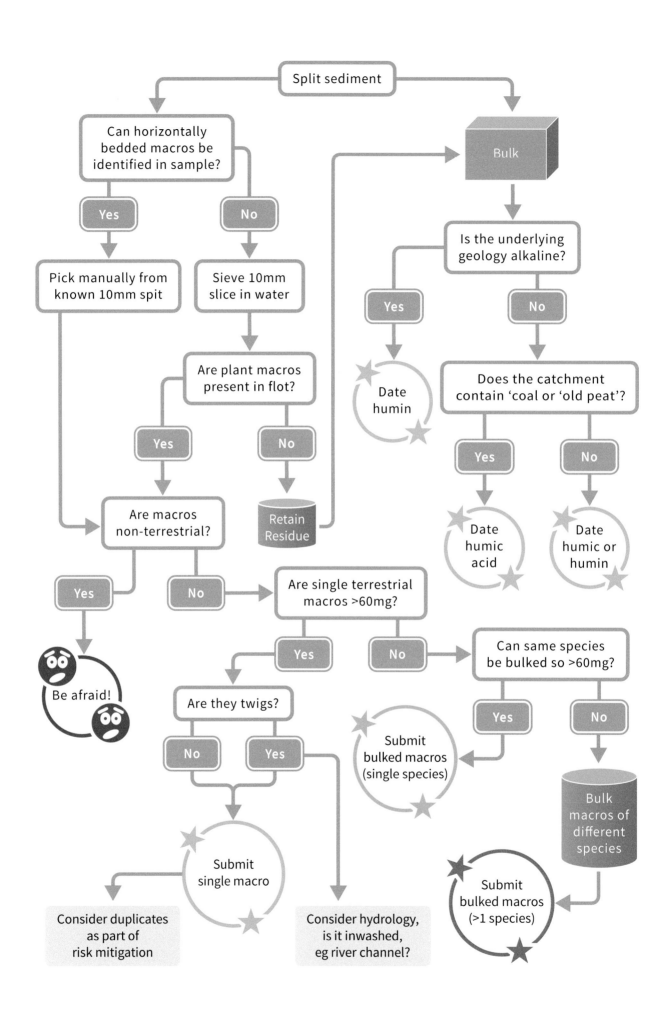

Split sediment

Can horizontally bedded macros be identified in sample?
- Yes → Pick manually from known 10mm spit
- No → Sieve 10mm slice in water

Are plant macros present in flot?
- Yes
- No → Retain Residue

Are macros non-terrestrial?
- Yes → Be afraid!
- No → Are single terrestrial macros >60mg?

Bulk

Is the underlying geology alkaline?
- Yes → Date humin
- No → Does the catchment contain 'coal or 'old peat'?
  - Yes → Date humic acid
  - No → Date humic or humin

Are single terrestrial macros >60mg?
- Yes → Are they twigs?
  - No → Submit single macro → Consider duplicates as part of risk mitigation
  - Yes → Consider hydrology, is it inwashed, eg river channel?
- No → Can same species be bulked so >60mg?
  - Yes → Submit bulked macros (single species)
  - No → Bulk macros of different species → Submit bulked macros (>1 species)

If dating is still considered to be merited, then it is be desirable to obtain large bulk sediment samples (which can be homogenised before dating). Can test pits be dug, or an open section sampled? If coring is necessary, can a wide-diameter corer with sleeved liners reach the required depth? If this is not possible, then it is necessary to proceed on the basis of the quantity of sediment available. If the amount of material at a given depth is large enough, it can be split and half sieved in water in an attempt to retrieve macrofossils for dating (the remainder surviving for bulk sediment dating and other analyses). The addition of chemicals such as calgon, sodium bi-carbonate, sodium hexametaphosphate, tetra sodium pyrophosphate decahydrate and hydrogen peroxide to sediment that is slow to disaggregate while wet sieving — to aid the identification of macrofossils — does not preclude their subsequent accurate radiocarbon dating. If only a very small amount of material is available, either the 10mm slice above or below the horizon of interest can be sieved to assess the likelihood that macrofossils will be found, or the horizon itself can be sieved in water and the residue retained for bulk dating if no macrofossils are recovered.

In theory, if the rationale for dating the **'humic acid'** and **'humin'** fractions of bulk organic sediment outlined above holds true in practice (*see* §3.2.2, fractions 3 and 4), then replicate measurements of these fractions on the same sample should usually be statistically consistent (ideally in 19 out of 20 cases). Reality is illustrated in Figure 24, where only 11 out of every 20 cases produce statistically consistent measurements. There is a clear tendency for the 'humic acid' fraction to be younger than the 'humin' fraction (on average by 86±4 BP). Where the two fractions of a sample give statistically consistent results, our confidence that the radiocarbon dates reflect the time of sediment accumulation is greater. But this

does not tell us which, if either, fraction accurately dates the deposition of the sediment, when the measurements on the two fractions diverge.

In selecting which fraction to target for dating, the geology and hydrology of the site are key. If the site is on an alkaline substrate (e.g. chalk), then there is a risk that results on humic acids will be anomalously young (especially if the sediment is early Holocene in age). Catchments with coal measures or older peat deposits that can be incorporated into sediments through erosion and run-off run the risk that results on the humin fraction can be anomalously old and thus dating the humic acids would be preferable. Whichever approach is adopted, adequate replication is essential (*see* §3.3.2). It should not be necessary to date the **total organic fraction** (i.e. bulk the bulk fractions!) using AMS.

This discussion illustrates the difficulties of dating organic sediments. In most circumstances, accurate dating can be achieved, but it is necessary to carefully consider the context, geomorphology and stratigraphic relationships between replicate measurements in order to construct such chronologies and identify inaccurate dates. Samples of single waterlogged plant macrofossils are the material of choice and, where necessary, these can be bulked together to provide sufficient material for dating. Figure 25 provides a flow diagram that can aid in these difficult site-specific choices.

Bone diagenesis
The burial environment also degrades bone samples. As collagen decays, its strands untwist and become vulnerable to contamination by humic acids. Laboratory pretreatment aims to retrieve **collagen** or clean gelatin for dating. This is particularly difficult for samples with low collagen levels, where most of the protein content of the bone has decayed, and so most laboratories utilise methods of assessing whether the protein is sufficiently well preserved for accurate dating (usually C:N ratios, %C, %N or percentage yield by weight). Generally, bone collagen preservation is higher in cortical bone (e.g. a femur) or in tooth dentine where the protein has been protected by the surrounding enamel.

Figure 25: Flow diagram to illustrate the steps needed when deciding which materials should be dated from organic sediment (image by J. Vallender).

Collagen preservation of some bones, in England usually those from sites on acid substrates, is simply not adequate for radiocarbon dating. But even on these sites, a small proportion of bones could be better preserved owing to local variations in the burial environment. In these cases, it can be worth pre-screening samples for protein preservation using %N measurements on whole bone (Brock et al. 2010a). This involves drilling a small amount of bone powder (c. 5mg, or a small pinch of salt) from each bone and measuring its %N content in a conventional mass spectrometer. Bones with more than 0.76%N have an 84% chance of successful dating. As no chemical pretreatment is required, costs are modest, and so large numbers of bones can be pre-screened so that the small proportion that are datable can be identified. Recently an entirely non-destructive technique, near-infrared spectroscopy, has been shown to similarly assess the collagen content of bone samples (Sponheimer et al. 2019).

Dating collagen from charred bone does not usually produce accurate radiocarbon dates. This is because the charring process in effect accelerates the degradation of bone collagen and makes it particularly susceptible to contamination by humic acids. Similarly, bone apatite that has been insufficiently **calcined** can also produce inaccurate results. This can be assessed on the basis of colour before submission for dating: white calcined bone should be selected in preference to grey or blackened material. In the dating laboratory a variety of tests can also be employed — the organic content of the sample, the crystallinity index or the splitting factor — to assess the suitability of a sample for accurate dating (Van Strydonck et al. 2010).

Anthropogenic contamination
The contamination so far discussed derives from the natural environment, but we also have to consider anthropogenic sources of contamination. Some of these are unavoidable, such as samples derived from ground contaminated by past industrial uses or timber that has undergone wood treatment during past structural maintenance; others are introduced accidently by archaeologists, such as fuel leaks from on-site generators or water-pumps; and still others are

introduced inadvertently by archaeologists during sample retrieval, processing, storage, packaging and conservation.

Obviously, it is better if a sample is not contaminated in the first place. But where such material does need to be dated, the critical factors are the nature of the material to be dated and the type of contaminant present. Situations where the contaminant is chemically the same as the sample to be dated are the most problematic (for example, modern cigarette ash in carbonised plant material, animal-bone glue coating bones, or algae growing on waterlogged plant remains). It is also difficult to deal with samples that are contaminated by unspecific cocktails of chemicals, such as IMS. It is, however, often possible to at least attempt to date samples that have undergone consolidation with Polyvinyl Acetate (PVA) or cellulose nitrate (for bones) or Polyethylene Glycol (PEG) (for waterlogged wood). There will always be more concern about the reliability of a radiocarbon date on a contaminated sample than would be the case for an uncontaminated sample. A larger sample is often required, and the laboratory procedures necessary are aggressive and non-trivial. Where such contamination is suspected, it is essential that as much information as possible is gathered about the chemical(s) that might have been used, and that the proposed analysis is discussed with the radiocarbon dating facility before samples are submitted.

3.3 Statistical simulation and sample selection

Sample selection needs to balance the risks of dating a sample or series of samples, against the probability of achieving the objectives of the dating programme. The aim is to minimise the risk and the cost of the dating programme, while maximising the information gain. Sometimes suitable samples are not available, and the temptation to submit inferior material for dating should be resisted. Dates on such samples almost always mislead more than they inform, and hamper the understanding of past chronologies (e.g. Darvill and Wainwright 2009).

3.3.1 How many samples?

First, you need to estimate how many samples you need to date to achieve the objective of the dating programme to the desired resolution. This is done by running a series of simulations covering a representative range of the likely outcomes of the dating programme.

The following needs to be defined:

■ the prior information relevant to the problem that can be included in the model (*see* §2.2.1);

■ the pool of samples that are potentially suitable for dating (*see* §3.2), and their relationships to that prior information;

■ the error terms that are likely to be returned by the selected radiocarbon facility, given the likely age and material of the samples to be submitted; and

■ a representative range of scenarios for the likely actual calendar dating of the problem under consideration.

For site-based studies a Harris matrix of the samples that are potentially suitable for dating, or a schematic diagram showing them with the site phasing, is often helpful. This information then needs to be combined into a simulation model.

These are of variable complexity. This may simply involve simulation of a single date. For example,

is it worth dating a carbonised food residue on a pottery sherd that is typologically known to be 'early Anglo-Saxon' (*c.* AD 420–700)? We can simulate the calibrated date we would get if we submit a single sample from this residue for radiocarbon dating (Fig. 26). In this case, the inputs into the simulation are our expected dating and an anticipated error on an AMS measurement of this age of about ±25 BP. This simulation illustrates two points. Firstly, it tells us that we can expect much better precision (to within a century) if the sample is later 6th or 7th century. If the sample is earlier than this, then a radiocarbon date will simply tell us that the sherd was used in the 5th or early 6th century AD. Archaeological judgement will tell us whether this precision is useful for the problem under consideration. Secondly, it shows the risks of submitting single samples. Simply from the expected statistical scatter on radiocarbon dates, some of the time the actual dates of a sample will lie on the limits of a calibrated radiocarbon date (e.g. the simulation at AD 460, where the true date actually lies on one of the smaller, later humps of the probability distribution rather than on the larger hump in the early 5th century). Potentially, single dates can mislead.

To take a slightly more complex example, we have a small, single-phase, late Iron Age farmstead and would like to know, to within a century, when it was occupied and for how many generations. Bone is not preserved, so we are reliant on dating carbonised plant remains from a variety of fired features on the farmstead. How many samples do

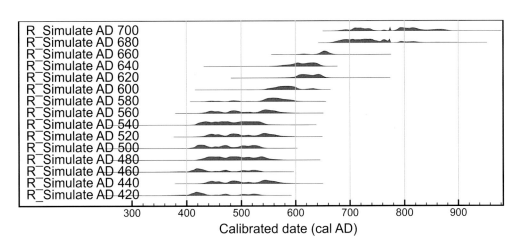

Figure 26: Simulated radiocarbon dates for actual ages from AD 420 to AD 700 (with error terms on the radiocarbon measurements of ±25BP), illustrating the effect of the calibration curve (Reimer et al. 2020) on calibrated radiocarbon dates (image by A. Bayliss).

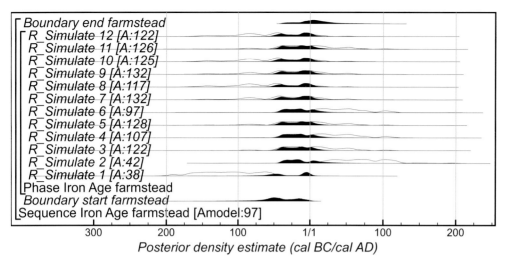

Figure 27: Probability distributions of simulated dates from a late Iron Age farmstead, derived from a chronological model incorporating a uniform distribution for the use of the settlement. The large square brackets down the left-hand side of the diagram, along with the OxCal keywords, define the overall model exactly (http://c14.arch.ox.ac.uk/) (image by A. Bayliss).

we need to date to obtain the required resolution? In this case, our prior information is that all the samples derive from a period between when the farmstead was established and when it was abandoned. We have many potential short-life, single-entity samples, which should provide error terms of about ±30 BP by AMS. Say, the site was occupied for 40 years in the last decades of the 1st century BC and we take two samples from each of six fired features (i.e. 12 samples in total). We get a model of the form shown in Figure 27.

This tells us that the site was established in *105 cal BC–cal AD 5* (*95% probability*; *start farmstead*; Fig. 27). This range covers 110 years and includes

the actual date input into the simulation (40 BC). It estimates that the site ended in *45 cal BC–cal AD 65* (*95% probability*; *end farmstead*; Fig. 27). This range also covers 110 years and also includes the actual date input into the simulation (1 BC). In neither case does the model estimate the key parameters to the desired level of precision. So, we add two more simulated dates from another feature and rerun the model to see how far the precision obtained improves. Ultimately, we can plot the bandwidth of the date range obtained for each key parameter given different numbers of dated samples (Fig. 28). In this case, we can see that the desired level of precision for this application is achieved by obtaining dates on 14 samples.

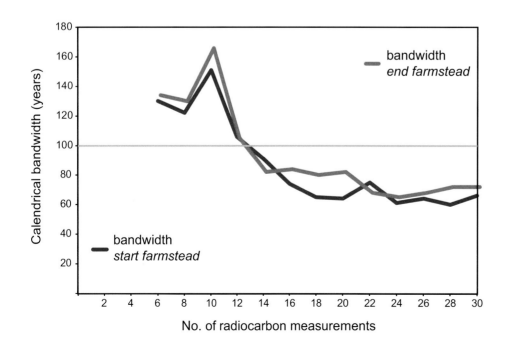

Figure 28: Calendrical bandwidth of the Highest Posterior Density intervals for the start farmstead and end farmstead parameters from a series of simulations for the chronology of the fictitious late Iron Age farmstead with increasing numbers of radiocarbon dates. This farmstead was in use for 40 years from 40 BC to 1 BC. The models are of the form shown in Figure 27. The red line denotes the desired precision for this application (image by A. Bayliss).

Of course, we do not actually know that this site was used for 40 years between 40 BC and 1 BC. It could have been used for 40 years between 80 BC and 40 BC, or for 20 years between 70 BC and 50 BC, or for 80 years between 100 BC and 20 BC, etc. So, we need to produce a series of simulations for different scenarios and a series of graphs of the form of Figure 27 (which itself summarises 13 simulation models). In this case, we might perhaps need to build 150–200 simulation models (which would take an experienced modeller perhaps half a day). This will give us an idea of the variation in the number of samples that we might need to achieve the required precision for this application; perhaps, in the best-case scenario, we would only need 12 samples, but in the worst-case scenario we would need 20.

We now need to consider how to use this information to inform our sampling strategy. Simulation is only a guide to the number of samples that, statistically, are needed to achieve an objective. Archaeological factors also need to feed into the strategy. There might, for example, be seven structures in the farmstead, each of which has a hearth or other fired feature. Perhaps in this case we might suggest that dating two samples from one feature in each building would be sensible. A sampling strategy should be archaeologically representative as well as statistically viable.

Practical considerations also come into play. If minimising costs is paramount, we might submit 12 samples as a first round of dating, obtain and model the results, and then obtain another six samples, if necessary, in a second round (Fig. 11). This might, if the site actually falls on the most favourable part of the calibration curve investigated by our simulations, save us the cost of six radiocarbon dates. But it might also save us nothing and extend the post-excavation programme by several months. This might, in itself, be more costly than the potential saving in radiocarbon dating costs, and so it might be most cost-effective to submit 20 samples in the first round.

Generally, at least two rounds of dating are recommended for all but the simplest of applications. Because of the difficulties of dating sequences of organic sediments (see §3.2.1, §3.2.2 and §3.3.2), two rounds of dating are essential in these cases. A preliminary round of dating is needed to demonstrate that a reliable chronology can be obtained from the sediments, and then further dating is needed to construct the chronology. Commissioning of extensive palaeoenvironmental analysis should normally follow the first stage of dating. For complex or large-scale applications, three rounds of dating should be scheduled as optimal.

In other cases, simulation might lead to the decision not to proceed with an intended programme of radiocarbon dating. For example, if this application fell on a different part of the calibration curve, and simulation suggested that no matter how many samples were submitted the maximum precision obtainable was to within 200 years, and we already know the date of the site to this resolution, then there is no point proceeding with the dating. Or, if simulation suggested that we needed between 40 and 50 samples to achieve useful precision, and we only have 30 potential samples, then we cannot proceed. Or we might decide that the archaeological objective of dating this site to within 100 years does not merit the cost of 50 radiocarbon dates.

This scenario might lead us to recast our objective into something that is less ambitious, but achievable; or it might lead us to think about the objective from a different angle. Do we really want to date the farmstead? Or is what is important actually the regional typology of ceramic forms? Could we use the typological series of the pottery to provide constraints on our model? Sometimes we do not even date what we are interested in to achieve our objective, but rather think laterally. A good example is dating field systems, where often the most effective strategy is to date one set of features that are cut by the field ditches, and another set that overlie the silted-up system. Samples from within the field ditches themselves are often both scarce and residual (Griffiths et al. 2021).

What is important in all these cases is that we have made an informed decision based on what can be achieved given the datable material and prior information that is available. There is no point in submitting 10 suitable samples for dating to achieve an objective that requires 20 samples. The objective will not have been achieved and resources will have been wasted. But if we decide to reallocate resources within a project to fund 25 radiocarbon dates that simulation suggests are needed to resolve reliably an important archaeological question, we can do so in the knowledge that this expenditure will have a good chance of achieving the required chronology.

The exception to this is where dating is undertaken to contribute to a wider research objective highlighted in a national or regional research agenda. For example, if there is a regional priority to date Beaker pottery, then dating two samples from a pit containing diagnostic Beaker sherds will ultimately contribute to wider understanding (for example, of the time-transgressive nature of the appearance of this ceramic style across England), even though the pit itself is only dated to a resolution of within a few hundred years.

3.3.2 Mitigating risk

So far, we have inhabited a paradise where all samples date the **target event** intended and all measurements are accurate to within their quoted uncertainty. The real world is not like this. Few radiocarbon samples, and even fewer sampling strategies, are perfect. There is always some element of risk in dating a group of samples, but we aim to minimise this and, if possible, to mitigate it.

This is done by testing the accuracy of the radiocarbon dates obtained, both individually and as a group. Our sampling strategy must consider both the risks posed by archaeological weaknesses in our pool of samples and the risks posed by their scientific complexities. There are a number of methods that we can use as a check on our results:

■ the coherence of a suite of related radiocarbon dates — are there any clear **outliers** or **misfits**? (see §2.2.2);

■ the compatibility of a series of results with the relative chronological sequence known from archaeological information (such as stratigraphy); and

■ the consistency of replicate results on the same or similar material.

The first two methods come into play once our radiocarbon results have been reported; replicate samples, however, must be selected as part of the overall sampling strategy. Replication is neither scientific prurience nor an expensive luxury, but rather an essential element of any competent sampling strategy for radiocarbon dating.

There are two types of replicate measurement: multiple samples on different single-entities from the same context or feature, and replicate measurements on the same single-entity. The first mitigates the archaeological risk that the dated samples are residual, reworked or intrusive; the second mitigates the scientific risks of dating certain types of material.

The number of repeat samples that are needed to address archaeological concerns about the dated samples is directly related to the certainty of the relationship between the **dated event** and the **target event** (see §3.2.2). Basically, the greater the uncertainty of association, the greater the number of repeat samples needed. The number of repeat samples is also related to the other checks, if any, that we have on the dates. So, for example, if there is a sequence of ten contexts each containing articulating animal bones, the stratigraphy will check the reliability of the measurements and so replicates will not be required. If, however, the sequence is ten levels in an organic sediment and the samples are waterlogged plant macrofossils, then two or three replicate pairs of single-entity macrofossils from the same level would be ideal to check for reworking. If the ten samples have no stratigraphic controls but are, for example, the base of basal sedimentation across a region, then replicate macrofossils from a higher proportion of the samples would be needed.

Generally, on archaeological grounds, a modest number of repeat measurements are needed on articulating or refitting samples, and on samples from structural material; but much higher numbers are needed for samples of disarticulated bone or carbonised plant remains, particularly as the putative functional association between the datable material and the context from which it was recovered becomes more uncertain. So, for example, when dating our fictional Iron Age farmstead, two samples might be sufficient from a hearth, but two samples might be needed from each of several postholes of a building. The highest level of repeat sampling is needed in dating organic sediments, particularly when submitting a first set of samples from a sequence to determine whether it can be dated reliably. In this case a good rule of thumb is that samples of waterlogged plant material should be sought every 0.5m through the part of the sequence that is of interest, and that half of the levels dated should have replicate samples.

Replicate measurements undertaken to address the scientific complexities of dated samples are generally repeat determinations taken on the same sample, or on different fractions of the same sample. Most radiocarbon laboratories have continuing programmes of random replication that are part of their internal quality assurance procedures, and that form part of their protocols for error calculation. Most scientific replicates commissioned by archaeologists are therefore likely to consist either of repeat measurements of different fractions of the same sample, or on samples that are split and dated by two different radiocarbon facilities.

In this case the degree of replication needed depends on the other checks that are available on the accuracy of the results, on the scientific difficulty of producing reproducible measurements on the material (Bayliss and Marshall 2019, table 1) and on the importance of the application. In an extreme example (see §5.2), replicate measurements were made by each of two different laboratories. Generally, some degree of inter-laboratory replication is wise for contaminated or poorly-preserved samples. In larger studies, and where sufficient material is available, it could also be merited for bones and charred food residues on pottery sherds. For some types of sample, for example when dating lime mortar, repeat measurements are an integral part of the dating process. If bulk organic sediment must be dated, then measurement of humic acid and humin replicates should be the norm, at least for the first set of samples from a sequence used to determine whether reliable dating is feasible. In this case replicate measurements should be obtained every 0.5m through the part of the sequence that is of interest.

Replicate measurements might also be needed to check for radiocarbon offsets. Where samples of articulated herbivore bone and articulated human bone occur in the same inhumation, it is important that radiocarbon determinations are obtained on both the human and the animal. This **perfect pair** will provide a check for a **dietary offset** in the human bone. Similarly, to check for the incorporation of an **old-wood offset** from pyre fuel in **calcined** bone, when dating cremation deposits replicate, measurements on a **single-entity**, short-life carbonised plant macrofossil and a fragment of white, calcined bone are desirable.

A sampling strategy for radiocarbon dating should consider all the factors discussed in §3.3. Simulation models will provide an indication of the number of samples that could be needed, given the shape of the relevant portion of the calibration curve and archaeological prior information that can be incorporated in the chronological model. Other things being equal, fewer radiocarbon dates will be needed where there are more archaeological constraints on the model. Identifying this prior information and suitable samples that enable it to be exploited is thus extremely cost-effective. Theoretical simulation models are helpful, but need to be interpreted intelligently. A sampling strategy also needs to be representative of the archaeological remains that are being dated, and sufficient replication needs to be commissioned to mitigate risks in the archaeological or scientific characteristics of the proposed samples.

Designing an efficient and effective radiocarbon sampling strategy from the mass of datable material from a site is undoubtedly the most difficult and technically demanding step in the Bayesian process. But it is key, and so commissioning a specialist to undertake this work is likely to be worthwhile in all but the simplest of cases.

3.4 Purchasing radiocarbon dates

Having determined which samples should be submitted for dating, the next step in the Bayesian process is to submit the samples for dating to a radiocarbon laboratory.

Best practice is to split the samples from a site between two different laboratories. This provides a degree of cross-checking that will ensure the reproducibility and accuracy of the radiocarbon measurements and the resultant chronology. It also mitigates the risks inherent in any complex scientific process, and is essential when high-precision dating is required. In some circumstances, however, this risk will have to be weighed against the practicalities of the project timetable and funding.

You should consider any technical constraints that the samples could impose. Are any of the samples of less routine materials that not all laboratories accept for dating? Are your samples contaminated, or particularly small? Is the quoted precision critical to the success of your dating programme? Information on these issues is often available from laboratory websites, date-lists or publications (*see* Appendix). For non-routine or contaminated samples, it is certainly worth contacting the laboratory to discuss a potential submission before sending the samples.

Quality is also an essential consideration. The technical procedures used by laboratories should be fully published, and thus accessible to future generations of researchers who need to trace these details. Laboratories should use internationally recognised reference materials (the results of which are sometimes reported along with your results), and take part in the series of international radiocarbon inter-comparison exercises (most

recently SIRI; Scott et al. 2017). Laboratories should also have their own, internal quality assurance procedures, the results of which are often published. A full list of radiocarbon laboratories is maintained by the journal *Radiocarbon* (http://www.radiocarbon.org/Info/Labs.pdf).

Other considerations affecting the choice of radiocarbon laboratory are practical. Most laboratories can provide an indication of the likely timescale for the provision of radiocarbon results on submission of samples. Some will guarantee a turn-around time, and offer 'express' services for situations where time is of the essence. Ultimately the reliability of laboratories in producing results within the timescale indicated is best assessed by experience.

Costs are another consideration. These can be found on the relevant laboratory websites, but care must be taken to determine what taxes (e.g. VAT) are liable for a particular project. Many laboratories offer bulk discounts (and even loyalty cards!) for 'persistent customers', and so it may be worth organising the submission of radiocarbon samples centrally in your organisation to maximise the advantage of such discounts. Express services are typically considerably more expensive.

Care must be taken to determine which associated measurements will be undertaken by each laboratory. For archaeological samples from England, $\delta^{13}C$ values should be obtained routinely. You should check which type of $\delta^{13}C$ value will be measured and reported by a laboratory (*see* §1.4) and determine whether this is a standard part of the reported measurement or whether extra charges apply. If additional associated measurements are required, such as C:N ratios or IRMS $\delta^{13}C$ and $\delta^{15}N$ values, these might be provided by the dating laboratory (usually at additional cost), but might have to be sourced elsewhere.

It is essential that all permissions for destructive analysis and export/import permits are obtained before samples are despatched. Human remains will require relevant permission (Mays et al. 2013, 4). Certain archaeological objects of more than 50 years in age might require an export licence (http://www.artscouncil.org.uk/what-we-do/supporting-museums/cultural-property/export-controls/export-licensing/). Samples from endangered species sent to laboratories outside the UK will require an export permit (https://www.gov.uk/cites-imports-and-exports/). Samples destined for laboratories in some countries might require specific import documentation, which will be supplied by the relevant laboratory.

All samples should be fully documented before submission for dating, and laboratories generally have procedures for this purpose. Radiocarbon dates are expensive, and it is worth double-checking that the labelling on the samples and the accompanying documentation is consistent.

Samples should consist of exactly what you want the radiocarbon laboratory to measure, and generally material can be sub-sampled for radiocarbon dating by specialists on the project team. For example, if you have a number of cereal grains from a context, select a large, well-preserved grain, obtain as precise a botanical identification as possible, photograph it, and send that single grain in a glass vial to the laboratory to be dated. Do not send multiple grains, as the laboratory will not necessarily know that you want a single-entity to be dated, and might bulk them together for analysis. If the selected grain is too small, the laboratory will contact you for a replacement.

It can be difficult to judge whether waterlogged plant macrofossils are large enough for dating. If there is choice, then the largest terrestrial single entity should be selected. If this is unlikely to make up the weight required by the relevant laboratory, then advice should be sought on how much material is needed. Judgement is required, as the risks of bulking together more than one item for dating (see §3.2.2) have to be balanced against the risk of a sample failing, or producing an inaccurate result, if insufficient material is supplied.

Some materials are better sub-sampled in the radiocarbon laboratory, however, particularly if specialist knowledge is needed to select the best material for dating. Carbonised food crusts on pottery should generally be left on the sherd. This should be sent to the laboratory, where the residue will be sub-sampled for dating and the object will be returned to the submitter. Sub-sampling intact bones for radiocarbon dating requires specialist drilling equipment (such as that used for sampling for stable isotopic studies; Fig. 29). If this is not available, complete bones can be sent for dating to be sub-sampled in the radiocarbon dating laboratory, which will again be returned to the submitter.

Samples should be stored as described above (see §3.2.1), although additional packaging is usually required for samples that are to be sent by post (special delivery) or courier. It is important that samples of carbonised material are not crushed (smaller fragments tend to produce lower yields of carbon during laboratory processing), and it is important that glass vials do not break during transport. Generally, packing in bubble-wrap or polystyrene chippings in a sturdy box is optimal.

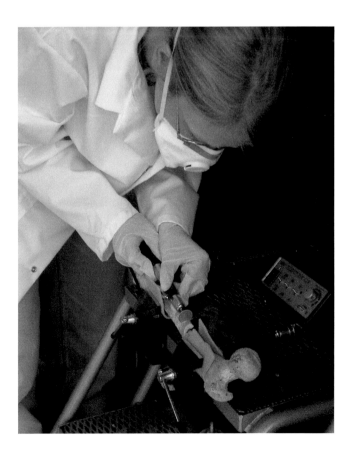

Figure 29: Sampling a bone for radiocarbon dating (© Historic England).

3.5 Preliminary modelling and additional samples

When the radiocarbon results are reported, they replace the simulated measurements in the simulation model. Almost always the real results will not be quite as anticipated. Most commonly it will be the assessment of the taphonomy of the dated sample that will be in error. Sometimes samples will be residual or intrusive, and it will be necessary to revisit the chain of inference by which the association of the dated sample to the archaeological event of interest was assessed before its submission for dating. On other occasions, it is necessary to reconsider the prior archaeological information that has been included in a model. Direct stratigraphic relationships usually prove to be secure, but the criteria on which dated deposits have been phased often require re-evaluation. Occasionally, something will have gone wrong with a radiocarbon measurement in the laboratory and it will be necessary to ask for the technical details of a sample to be reviewed.

Once these problems have been identified and re-modelled in an appropriate way, further simulated dates are added to the existing suite of radiocarbon dates. Once the additional number of samples needed has been determined (*see* §3.3.1), further samples are selected from the pool of potential samples that has already been identified (*see* §3.2.2 and §3.2.3) or are chosen because further replication to assess sample taphonomy or laboratory accuracy is required (*see* §3.3.2). These are dated and the cycle repeats (Fig. 11). Ideally, this process repeats until adding more simulated dates does not materially improve the precision of the chronology produced by the model. In practice, however, usually either there is no more money for more samples, or the post-excavation timetable cannot accommodate further rounds of sampling. Occasionally, there is be no further suitable material for dating.

This process is time-consuming; frequently as much staff time is spent in selecting samples and running simulations as is spent in analysis and publication of the final set of results. However, projects where the samples are selected around the model, rather than where the model is grafted onto an existing series of dates, have consistently provided much more precise chronologies and have been much more cost-effective and archaeologically useful.

3.6 Reporting radiocarbon dates and chronological models

The detailed reporting of radiocarbon dates and chronological models is a fundamental part of any programme of radiocarbon dating.

3.6.1 Reporting radiocarbon dates

Details of the radiocarbon measurements, the methods used to produce them and the samples analysed will be essential information for future generations of researchers. Currently any synthetic study of English chronology requires considerable research to track down the relevant details. Often the original reporting documentation sent by the radiocarbon facility can be traced in project archives, and radiocarbon laboratories generally do their best to help trace details of past measurements. But accessing primary archives is time-consuming, and over time radiocarbon facilities do close. There are also potential legal and other barriers to radiocarbon dating laboratories making information available (for example, client confidentiality in perpetuity is a condition for ISO-9000 accreditation).

The following information must be published for each radiocarbon measurement:

■ Details of the facility or facilities that produced the results, and how samples were pretreated, prepared for measurement and dated. References to published papers should be preferred to citation of web addresses (as the archival stability of the latter is currently unproven). This information should be supplied by the radiocarbon dating facilities.

Example: Samples of bulk peat were pretreated using an acid-base-acid protocol (Mook and Waterbolk 1985) and then converted to benzene and dated by liquid scintillation spectrometry at the University of Waikato (Hogg et al. 1987). The

Laboratory number	Sample details [see Table 4]	Radiocarbon Age (BP)	δ¹³C (AMS) (‰)	δ¹³C (IRMS) (‰)	δ¹⁵N (IRMS) (‰)	C:N (atomic)	Calibrated date (95% probability)	Highest Posterior Density interval (95% probability)
OxA-14770	Sample 1	4802±35		−20.7	+10.1	3.3		3625–3620 cal BC (1%) or 3615–3525 cal BC (94%)
GrA-30885	Sample 2	4910±40		−22.4				3705–3635 cal BC
GrA-23933	Sample 3	5105±45		−20.4				3955–3810 cal BC
OxA-15390	Sample 4	4874±33		−27.1				3710–3630 cal BC
OxA-14608	Sample 5A	3445±31						
SUERC-6143	Sample 5B	3495±35						
Weighted mean	T'=1.1; v=1; T'(5%)=3.8	3467±23					1880–1695 cal BC	
Beta-245426	Sample 6	1130±60		−28.0				cal AD 900–1025
OxA-11828	Sample 7	8785±45		−22.8				7835–7720 cal BC
UB-3792	Sample 8	4365±18		−22.9±0.2				3020–2920 cal BC
SUERC-10179	Sample 9	1475±35		−27.2				cal AD 630–655
NZA-18502	Sample 10	4668±40		−25.0				3625–3370 cal BC
OxA-13318	Sample 11	5222±31		−19.8			4210–3970 cal BC	
GrA-25546	Sample 12	4765±40		−22.2				3605–3495 cal BC (61%) or 3455–3375 cal BC (34%)
BM-640	Sample 13	1425±45		−25.0 (assumed)				
KIA-27624	Sample 14	4779±40	−25.7					3630–3525 cal BC
HAR-7021	Sample 15	2600±90		−27.1			960–440 cal BC	
OxA-13135	Sample 16	4950±100		−30.6				3920–3765 cal BC
SUERC-9110	Sample 17	2800±35		−25.6				1050–835 cal BC
OxA-5349	Sample 18	1530±50		−20.2			cal AD 420–640	
SUERC-44444	Sample 19	7347±27		−31.1			6330–6080 cal BC	
Wk-35929	Sample 20A	9553±43		−27.6				
Wk-35923	Sample 20B	9689±42		−28.8				
Weighted mean	T'=5.1; v=1; T'(1%)=6.4	9623±31					9220–8840 cal BC	
HAR-4527	Sample 21	2110 ±80		−24.2			360 cal BC–cal AD 80	
HAR-3464	Sample 22	1280±80		−0.5			cal AD 810–1350	

Table 3: Reporting radiocarbon and stable isotope measurements.
The exact format of this table should vary according to circumstances. Greyed out cells indicate information that is often, but not invariably, required (see text). Samples have been calibrated using the probability method (Stuiver and Reimer 1993) and the atmospheric calibration curve for the northern hemisphere (Reimer et al. 2020), except for HAR-3464, which has been calibrated using the marine calibration curve (Heaton et al. 2020) and a ΔR value of −179 ± 93 BP calculated from the 10 closest marine reservoir datapoints to the location of the find (http://calib.org/marine/; Reimer and Reimer 2017). Posterior density estimates are taken from models defined in Bayliss et al. (2020, supplementary information 3; samples 1 and 14), Figure 65 (samples 2 and 4), Bayliss et al. (2020, supplementary information 3; samples 3 and 16), Ingham (2011, fig .18; sample 6), Bayliss et al. (2007b, fig .6.2; sample 7), Marshall et al. (2012, fig. 7; sample 8), Best and Gent (2007, illus 24; sample 9); Whittle et al. (2011, figs 8.27–9; sample 10; figs 3.8–11; sample 12), Bayliss et al. (2013, fig. 6.52; sample 13), and Johnson and Waddington (2008, illus 27; sample 17), recalculated using IntCal20 where appropriate.

other samples were pretreated and combusted as described by Brock et al. (2010b), and then graphitised and dated by AMS at the Oxford Radiocarbon Accelerator Unit (Dee and Bronk Ramsey 2000; Bronk Ramsey et al. 2004a).

- Details of the radiocarbon results and associated measurements and how these have been calculated.

Example: The results are conventional radiocarbon ages (Stuiver and Polach 1977) and are listed in

Sample	Sample details ☺
Sample 1	ws8, human bone, right femur from adult male, partially articulated skeleton group 7, overlying ws13 in primary mortuary deposit
Sample 2	cattle right ulna articulating with radius from Segment 3, F-1672=F44 Context 59; fill of an early recut, stratigraphically later than Sherd Group 265
Sample 3	AB1 (511), wild boar tibia with refitting unfused epiphysis from Pit F7
Sample 4	Sherd Group 98, carbonised residue on 1 large body sherd among >10 from a single Neolithic bowl from Segment 2, F1358, Context 1272; lowest fill of recut of segment
Sample 5A	calcined human bone from Cremation Burial [7074] of an adult ?male individual
Sample 5B	replicate of Sample 5A
Sample 6	waterlogged wood, Prunus sp. roundwood sail from Well Lining in [5288]
Sample 7	single carbonised hazelnut shell fragment from hearth [293]
Sample 8	antler pick from bottom of ditch in Cutting 25.2
Sample 9	Polygonum aviculare seeds (×20) from fill [691] of plank-lined springhead
Sample 10	single fragment of charred hazelnut shell from Pit 5025, which contained plain and decorated bowl pottery, struck flint, charcoal, charred plant remains, and animal bone
Sample 11	AB12 (450), paired dog left and right mandibles from secondary barrow, cutting DX
Sample 12	fragment of one of three interleaved proximal rib fragments from a large mammal found together in outer ditch, Bone Group 115 in top of Layer 111
Sample 13	beeswax from lamp accompanying primary burial in Mound 1
Sample 14	ws14, human bone, right femur from adult, possibly female (no articulation demonstrable), from Bone Group Q in third layer of primary mortuary deposit
Sample 15	bulk charcoal, Corylus avellana and Pomoideae, from Context 61: gleyed colluvium with lenses of burnt material representing occupation activity that abuts or pre-dates Structure 57
Sample 16	PT1 AuW1976.217, Vessel 33, carbonised residue adhering to sherd from buried soil west of the midden in square m21
Sample 17	single fragment of charcoal, Corylus avellana, from Posthole 346 of Building 4
Sample 18	disarticulated cattle mandible from a layer of fine silt and chalk rubble sealing the layers of phase II, and probably originating as upcast from ditch cleaning of the monument, thus forming the third phase of the bank/rampart
Sample 19	W2, waterlogged Alnus glutinosa roundwood including bark, from prostrate tree on the surface of the peat
Sample 20A	W1, peat (200g), humic acid fraction, from 2cm spit at a depth of 16–18cm from the top of the peat
Sample 20B	W2, peat (200g), humin fraction, from 2cm spit at a depth of 16–18cm from the top of the peat
Sample 21	bulk sample of carbonised grain from Pit 277, Fill 278. A 4cm thick deposit of carbonised grain, covered the pit floor. The grain consisted mainly of spelt and six-row hulled barley. The grain was either burned within the pit or accumulated very rapidly. This sample came from the base of the deposit.
Sample 22	bulk sample of oyster shell (Ostrea sp.) from the top of the 3.4m oyster midden

Table 4: This page and opposite. Reporting sample details.

Table 3. The ages produced at Rijksuniversiteit Groningen have been calculated using the fractionation correction provided by the δ¹³C (AMS) values, which are not reported. Those produced at SUERC have been calculated using the reported δ¹³C values measured by conventional mass spectrometry.

■ Details of the material dated and the context from which it came (*see* Table 4).

The critical information that will be needed by future researchers, both to recalibrate your radiocarbon results as calibration data are

Sample details 😐	Sample details 🙁
femur from partially articulated skeleton in primary mortuary deposit	human bone from mortuary deposit
articulating animal bone from early recut of Segment 3	animal bone from ditch
juvenile wild boar tibia from Pit F7	animal bone from Pit 7 [Should be Pit F7?]
carbonised residue on Sherd Group 98 from lowest fill of recut in Segment 2	carbonised residue on sherd from ditch
human bone from Cremation [7074]	Cremation [7074]
human bone from Cremation [7074]	Cremation [7074]
Prunus sp. from Well Lining [5288]	Well Lining [5288]
hazelnut shell from hearth [293]	hazelnut shell from hearth
antler from ditch in Cutting 25.2	antler from ditch
waterlogged seeds from springhead	seeds from [691]
charred hazelnut shell from Pit 5025	hazelnut shell from Pit 5025
dog left mandible from secondary barrow	animal bone from secondary barrow
large mammal rib from outer ditch, layer 111	animal bone from outer ditch
beeswax from primary burial in Mound 1	beeswax from Mound 1
human femur from Bone Group Q in primary mortuary deposit	human bone from mortuary deposit
short-lived charcoal from occupation associated with or pre-dating Structure 57	charcoal from Context 61
residue on sherd from buried soil	pottery from buried soil
Corylus avellana from posthole of Building 4	charcoal from Building 4
cattle mandible from the third phase of the bank/rampart	animal bone from the bank
W2, waterlogged *Alnus* sp. from peat	W2, waterlogged wood from peat
W1, peat (humic acid fraction) at a depth of 16–18cm from the top of the peat	W1, peat from a depth of 16–18cm
W2, peat (humin fraction) at a depth of 16–18cm from the top of the peat	W2, peat from a depth of 16–18cm
carbonised grain from base of Pit 277, Fill 278	grain from Pit 277
oyster shell from the top of the midden	oyster shell from midden

refined and to re-interpret your data to answer new questions, is included under 1–3 and in Tables 3 and 4.

- Details of any replicate analyses, statistical tests on replicate groups of measurements, although sometimes more extensive discussion may be merited.

Example: Measurements on the humic acid and humin fractions of the large bulk peat sample are statistically consistent (GrN-28276, 1140±50 BP and GrN-28277, 1050±50BP; T'=1.6, T'(5%)=3.8, v=1; Ward and Wilson 1978) and so a weighted mean (1095±35 BP) has been calculated before calibration.

- Details of the calibration protocols used, including any reservoir corrections employed. Calibration is an essential step in the use of radiocarbon dating to infer chronology and this information will always be required.

Often, however, calibration is simply part of formal statistical modelling, and where further statistical analysis is undertaken, it might be more appropriate to provide posterior density estimates and Highest Posterior Density intervals (*see* §3.6.2), rather than simple calibrated date ranges.

In applications where no further analysis of the radiocarbon dates is undertaken, however — for example, when range finder dates are required — then calibrated radiocarbon dates should be reported.

Example: The quantile ranges of the calibrated dates for the samples given in Table 3 have been calculated using the probability method (Stuiver and Reimer 1993), and are quoted with end points rounded outwards to ten years. They have been calculated using OxCal v4.4 (Bronk Ramsey 2009a) and the current internationally-agreed atmospheric calibration dataset for the northern hemisphere, IntCal20 (Reimer et al. 2020). The sample of oyster shell (HAR-3464, 1280±80 BP) is from Poole, Dorset, and has been calibrated using the marine dataset of Heaton et al. (2020)

and a ΔR value of −179 ± 93 BP calculated from the ten closest marine reservoir datapoints to the site (http://calib.org/marine/; Reimer and Reimer 2017).

Replicate analysis and calibration are needed for the interpretation of the radiocarbon dates that have been obtained as part of a project. Both, however, can be reworked from the details provided under points 1– 3. and in Tables 3 and 4. As described in §1.6, calibration is not only now usually part of further analysis, but is also periodically refined, so it is essential that the information necessary for revising the calibrated dates and including them in future chronological models is provided.

In simple cases, the reporting of the radiocarbon dates in a project will be completed by the publication of the information in this section. In cases where Bayesian Chronological Modelling has been undertaken, however, the information in the following section should also be reported.

3.6.2 Reporting Bayesian chronological models
Bayesian chronological models are interpretative constructions. They will be revised, not only as calibration data and statistical methods improve, but also as archaeological understanding develops and new questions are posed. Consequently the aim of chronological modelling reporting is not just to explain how and why the models presented were constructed, but also to provide sufficient information to enable the reader to understand the strengths and weaknesses of those models, and so that they can be critically analysed and reconstructed by future researchers.

Chronological modelling reports should include the following information:

1. Objectives of the study
The objectives of the dating programme, including the dating precision needed to achieve these objectives and discussion of how the objectives may have been recast in the light of the available material, prior information, calibration curve, available funding, etc.

2. Methodology
This should include a statement of the approach adopted, including details of the radiocarbon calibration data (and any reservoir corrections), statistical methods and software used.

3. Sampling strategy
This should include discussion of:
a. the pool of potential samples available from the project (see §3.2.2 and §3.2.3),
b. the available prior information,
c. the results of any simulation models (see §3.3.1),
d. any other factors that affected the sampling strategy adopted (see §3.3.2), and
e. the rationale by which these elements have been combined into a strategy.

4. Details of scientific dates
Radiocarbon dates should be published as outlined in §3.6.1. Legacy data might also need to be reported to this level of detail, although reference to relevant publications might be adequate (depending on the quality of the original reporting). Where legacy data are reported in a variety of sources, it can be helpful to provide a table of dates (see Tables 3 and 4), so that readers can assess their quality.

Details of other scientific dates should be reported in a similar way (see Duller 2008, §9–10; English Heritage 2006, 18; English Heritage 1998, §2.7–8).

5. Model definition and description
It is essential that each model in a publication is explicitly defined so that it can be recreated by readers. Most published models have been created using one of the software packages listed in the Appendix, and can be defined as described in the relevant publication relating to that software (see Case Studies, §5). Sometimes, it is possible to define simple or variant models in the text. Models that have been constructed using new statistical procedures that have not been published elsewhere will need technical mathematical appendices.

Chronological models do not, however, simply have to be defined. They must also be justified. The prior information included in the model should be described, and its strengths and weaknesses assessed. Consideration should be given to whether the 'uninformative' prior information included is appropriate for the problem at hand, the robustness of the associations between the data and the prior information, and the identification of any outliers or misfits.

6. Sensitivity analyses
Having defined and justified a model, it is necessary to assess its strengths and weaknesses (see §2.2.2). Most usually this is done by varying components of a model to determine how sensitive the modelled chronology is to changes in the interpretations on which the modelling is based.

7. Recommendations for further work
Sometimes the assessment of the strengths and weaknesses of the current study, as described above will suggest or indicate that further work is needed.

The **posterior density estimates** produced by chronological models can be summarised using **Highest Posterior Density intervals**. These should be cited in italics to distinguish them from calibrated radiocarbon dates. They should be rounded outwards to a resolution that is dependent on that of the calibration curve used and the precision of the posterior distributions. All Highest Posterior Density intervals produced by a model should be rounded to the same resolution, which should not be greater than that of the relevant section of the calibration curve.

In practice, most **Highest Posterior Density intervals** are rounded outwards to five years, except for those from **wiggle-matching** on parts of the calibration curve that are interpolated at single-year resolution, which are rounded outwards to the nearest year.

3.6.3 Citation of Bayesian chronological models

Discussions of chronology often include comparisons between the dates of different sites and different artefacts. Rarely will all the relevant comparanda be included in the modelling for a project, and so it will often be necessary to cite key parameters from previously published models. It is essential that it is clear precisely which parameter is meant, and from which model it derives. Thus, in addition to the **Highest Probability Density interval**, both the parameter name and an exact reference to the published definition of the relevant model should be given.

For example, the building of the outer circuit of the Chalk Hill causewayed enclosure considered below would be cited as '*3760–3675 cal BC* (*95% probability*; *build outer Chalk Hill*; Bayliss and Marshall 2022, Fig. 65)'.

Key facts: reporting radiocarbon dates and Bayesian chronological models

For each radiocarbon date the unique laboratory identifier, the **conventional radiocarbon age** or **fraction modern** value, and the experimental uncertainty at 1σ must be reported, along with any associated measurements (e.g. $\delta^{13}C$ values). Details of the material dated and the context from which it came should be given, and the methods of sample preparation and measurement specified. Replicate analyses should be described, and details of the **calibration** procedures used should be given.

Reports on Bayesian chronological models should include descriptions of the objectives of the study, the methodology employed, and the sampling strategy adopted. The dated material and radiocarbon measurements should be fully described, as should the prior information included in the modelling. Each model must be explicitly defined so that it can be recreated. **Sensitivity analyses** are often required to assess the strengths and weaknesses of the models presented.

4 Project organisation and planning

Government guidance set out in the National Planning Policy Framework (NPPF) (Ministry of Housing, Communities and Local Government 2021) enshrines the principle of sustainable development in the planning process. Where archaeological projects are commissioned to inform the planning process the information sought should be proportionate to the significance of the heritage asset and the potential impacts of the proposed development. Assessments of heritage assets in advance of determinations of planning applications should therefore be sufficient to provide an understanding of the significance of heritage assets and their settings affected either directly or indirectly by the development proposals (e.g. desk-based assessment or field evaluation where appropriate).

4.1 Specifications and briefs

These guidelines are applicable to all archaeological projects, but are aimed primarily at those undertaken as part of the planning process. Providing an accurate estimate of costs for radiocarbon dating before a full assessment has been undertaken is inherently problematic. In cases where this is required, 'ring-fenced funds for scientific dating' in the overall budget should be identified. It is, however, much more satisfactory if projects adhere strictly to management principles, such as those outlined in MoRPHE (Historic England 2015c; Fig. 30), and post-excavations costs are identified as part of the assessment process.

For sites where radiocarbon dating can be expected to form an important part of a project (e.g. prehistoric sites, sites with waterlogged environmental remains) then specification of a fixed percentage of the overall tender for 'ring-fenced funds for scientific dating' would be prudent. The use of these funds would only take place following approval by the curator of costs resulting from the assessment. If, following assessment, the requirements for radiocarbon dating are not as extensive as envisaged, then not all the ring-fenced fund would be required. A practice such as this would encourage contractors to submit realistic tenders and thus avoid the tendency for very low post-excavation costs in project budgets.

Strategies for radiocarbon dating should be included in Project Designs and Written Schemes of Investigation. Definitions of briefs, specifications and project designs can be found in the Association of County Archaeological Officers (1993) *Model Briefs and Specifications for Archaeological Assessments and Field Evaluations* and the Chartered Institute for Archaeologists (CIfA) Standard and Guidance series (2014a–c; 2020a–d).

Curators who need further advice on the potential for using radiocarbon dating on specific sites can obtain independent non-commercial advice from Historic England (*see* Appendix). Where advice is obtained from a commercial contractor, it is the responsibility of the commissioning body to ensure that vested interests are openly declared, and that subsequent competition is fair (CIfA 2014c).

Specifications and briefs should ask for radiocarbon dating and chronological modelling to be carried out in accordance with these guidelines, and so Project Designs and Written Schemes of Investigation should include statements to this effect. Where relevant, named specialists should be included in such documents,

STAGES & ACTIVITIES	SCOPE	CONSIDERATIONS
PROJECT INITIATION		
Proposal, outline, research proposal Review point: Decision to proceed	Outlines broad requirements for work to be undertaken to ensure that it contributes to increased understanding and that it is appropriate/feasible. Provides an initial statement of aims, objectives and contributes to project proposals.	■ Contribute to aims and objectives. ■ Provide outline costings.
PROJECT PLANNING		
Specification, written scheme of investigation (WSI), research application, project design (PD), funding application Review point: authorise project	Details the proposed scheme of investigation and provides a benchmark for measuring the progress of the project. Describes aims, objectives and business case, togetherwith associated risk log and costs.	■ Ensure resources are appropriately costed. ■ Chronological modeller identified as part of the project team. ■ Radiocarbon laboratory(ies) identified. ■ Assess the chronological resource (known & unknown) and their signficance. ■ Input to specification/WSI/research proposal, etc, including research questions, sampling & retrieval methodologies. ■ Detail plans for dissemination and archiving of data and reports.
PROJECT EXECUTION		
Desk-based assessment (DBA) Review point	A programme of study of the historic environment within a specified area or site to address specific research aims and objectives. Scientific dating specialists should be consulted.	■ Review knowledge and understanding of the site's chronology. ■ Assess the potential signficance of the site.
Fieldwork (evaluation/ excavation/ historic building recording, etc) Review point	**Sample collection (field)** Evaluation identifies, defines the character, extent, quality and preservation of historic environment resource. Excavation (plus analagous forms of fieldwork) is more extensive and seeks to better understand the heritage resource.	■ Provide improved opportunities for the recovery of samples and better understanding of their contexts. ■ Ensure robust sample retrieval and storage. ■ Submisison of completely unexpected finds/ deposits lacking artefactual evidence for dating.
Assessment Review point	**Sample collection (off-site)** Assessment of potential samples for radiocarbon dating undertaken by appropriate specialists, eg zooarchaeologist, archaeobotanist, etc. Pre-screening bones for radiocarbon dating (eg %N content of whole bone). Collate prior information that will be included in the chronological modelling.	■ Ensure resources are appropriately costed. ■ Determine the potential of the pool of available samples to address the aims and objectives. ■ Undertake simulations. ■ Define number(s) of samples. ■ Liaise with other specialists. ■ Submit of samples for range-finder dating.
Analysis Review point	**Laboratory analaysis** Radiocarbon dating and stable isotope measurements undertaken by laboratory(ies).	■ Submit samples.
	Chronological modelling Analysis of radiocarbon dating and stable isotope results by chronological modeller/stable isotope specialists. Analysis, reporting and publication.	■ Build model. ■ Interpret model. ■ Consult with wider project team specialists. ■ Write narrative.
Dissemination & archive deposition Review point	**Archiving** Radiocarbon and stable isotope measurements togetherwith sample submission forms prepared and deposited for long-term storage.	■ Complete archiving tasks. ■ Return access material from laboratory(ies) to site archive.
PROJECT COMPLETION		
Closure	Make sure all tasks finished and products produced.	■ Reflect on the success/failure of steps taken and what can be learned to inform future projects.

and curators should ask for details of their relevant experience (published papers, reports, etc.), given that there is no formal means of accreditation.

Full use should be made of all available sources of information on the potential for using scientific dating effectively when planning archaeological projects. Chronology is the framework for understanding all archaeological sites and therefore the construction of reliable chronologies should form an integral part of the initial project specification. It should not be seen as a luxury.

4.2 Desk-based assessment

The purpose, definition and standard for desk-based assessment are given in CIfA (2020a). Specialists can contribute to desk-top assessments with information and evaluation of existing radiocarbon determinations from previous investigations, if they exist, and the potential for radiocarbon dating to contribute to the aims and objectives of the project. Such information can be used in order to help determine the location of evaluation trenches, and design appropriate sampling strategies.

4.3 Watching briefs

The purpose, definition and standard for watching briefs are given in CIfA (2020c). Radiocarbon dating undertaken on samples obtained during watching briefs would only be expected in exceptional circumstances (e.g. completely unexpected archaeological finds or deposits where artefactual evidence is absent).

4.4 Evaluation

The purpose, definition and standard for evaluations are given in CIfA (2014b). In order to understand the nature of the archaeological resource, evaluations are undertaken to inform decisions on planning and mitigation strategies. In some situations, an evaluation might be the only intervention undertaken. Radiocarbon dating as part of evaluations can therefore constitute an important contribution to understanding the archaeological resource.

Samples can be submitted to provide **range-finder dates** to help assess the significance of the archaeological resource. For example, radiocarbon dating might be used to answer questions such as:

- What is the age of unexpected discoveries?

- What is the age of deposits?

- What is the date of archaeological remains without diagnostic material culture?

The tight time constraints often applicable to assessment following evaluations must not mean that the rigorous principles outlined for radiocarbon sample selection (§3.2.2–3.2.3) are ignored.

Large-scale geoarchaeological coring programmes (Historic England 2015a) undertaken to understand buried deposits often include radiocarbon dating of range-finder samples. The utility of information derived from simply obtaining age estimates for the top and bottom of cores needs to be carefully considered and justified. Such an approach should only be undertaken where it can demonstrably be shown to contribute to the specific aims and objectives of the project.

Sometimes projects do not proceed beyond evaluation. In these cases, radiocarbon dates from key deposits can contribute to priorities identified in regional, period or national research agendas.

4.5 Excavation

Full excavation not only presents better opportunities for the recovery of samples for radiocarbon dating (e.g. Campbell et al. 2011), but more importantly enables better understanding their context. Samples should be retrieved and stored as outlined in §3.2.1, and it is important that site staff are aware of the necessary protocols. In selecting samples for radiocarbon dating, understanding of the taphonomic relationship between the datable material and the deposit from which it was retrieved is crucial (*see* §3.2.2), and the site recording should reflect this. For example, recording articulating groups of animal bone in the field is an extremely cost-effective strategy (Baker and Worley 2019, 18).

4.6 Assessment

An effective assessment for radiocarbon dating and chronological modelling can only be undertaken usefully once sufficient specialist assessments have been completed for the necessary information to be available: that is, the identification of the pool of potential samples for dating and the identification of the archaeological prior information that will be included in the chronological modelling (Fig. 11). This means that close co-operation among the radiocarbon/modelling specialist, site-director and other specialists is imperative to ensure the pertinent information is obtained. For example, it is not sufficient simply to equate the survival of organic remains with the potential for radiocarbon dating. The presence of suitable short-life single entity samples from an assessment of a proportion of samples by a wood specialist/archaeobotanist provides the level of detail required to make an informed radiocarbon dating assessment. Thus, specific assessment of the suitability of samples for radiocarbon dating (e.g. environmental remains) needs to be requested from the relevant specialists (*see* Campbell et al. 2011, 8). Generally, the assessment for scientific dating will be amongst the last programmed within this phase of the project.

An exception is pre-screening bones for radiocarbon dating using the %N content of whole bone (Brock et al. 2010a; 2012) — a rapid and inexpensive method only requiring 5–10mg of bone — as an indicator of collagen preservation (*see* §3.2.3).

As a minimum the following information is required by the specialist to carry out an assessment:

■ brief account of the nature and history of the site,

■ aims and objectives of the project,

■ summary of the archaeological results,

■ context types and stratigraphic relationships,

■ sample locations,

■ assessment reports from other relevant specialists, and

■ an idea of the project timetable and budget.

The primary aim of the assessment will be to ascertain the potential of the samples to address the aims and objectives of the project. In order to maximise resources, close consultation is required with other specialists involved in the project (e.g. dating objects for intrinsic interest that will also contribute to answering broader chronological questions). It is therefore best if all radiocarbon dating is co-ordinated by a single specialist.

The assessment report should contain:

■ aims and objectives of the project to which radiocarbon dating/chronological modelling can contribute,

■ specialist chronological aims and objectives,

■ a summary of potential samples,

- a summary of potential contexts to be assessed for samples suitable for dating,

- a statement of potential — how radiocarbon dating can contribute to site, specialist and wider research questions — simulation models if appropriate,

- recommendations for further work, including for full analysis if applicable, and

- the tasks, time and outline costings for future work (analysis and publication).

Given the potential expense of radiocarbon dating programmes, a staged-approach is recommended (*see* §3.1–3.3 and Fig. 11).

4.7 Post-excavation analysis

Radiocarbon dating and chronological modelling should have been planned and, as a minimum, outline costs provided while preparing the updated project design. The radiocarbon/ chronological modelling specialist will need to work closely with other specialists (e.g., the site director, radiocarbon laboratories, environmental archaeologists, osteologists, material culture specialists, and others) at all stages of the analysis.

The major part of the Bayesian process (Fig. 11) will be undertaken at this stage of the project (*see* §3.2–§3.5). It is essential that sufficient information and a timetable is available to enable the radiocarbon dating and chronological modelling programme to proceed in accordance with the overall project timetable. Forward planning is essential. Express radiocarbon dating is expensive and should not be used in compensation for inadequate project planning.

A full report should be provided in accordance with the guidance provided in §3.6.

4.8 Dissemination and archiving

4.8.1 Historic Environment Record (HER)
In accordance with current best practice reports on any archaeological intervention, even if only an evaluation, should be deposited with the local HER as quickly as possible following their completion and added to OASIS. Chronological information could form a component of these reports, including radiocarbon results. Radiocarbon dates, together with the results from other scientific dating methods, should be recorded on Historic Environment Records.

4.8.2 Publication
Where possible the report (*see* §3.6) should be included in the main body of the publication of a project (including in electronic supplementary information where this facility is available). But as it might not always be feasible to integrate the complete radiocarbon dating and chronological report with the full site publication, it might be appropriate for alternative publications in for example archaeological science, archaeological, environmental or other specialist journals.

4.8.3 Archiving
All radiocarbon dating certificates and radiocarbon and chronological modelling reports should be included in the material deposited with the archival body, in accordance with their standards. For published overall guidelines on archive deposition see Brown (2011), Longworth and Wood (2000), Museums and Galleries Commission (1992), Walker (1990), and Archaeological Data Service (1997; 2011).

Samples suitable for further dating are usually included within the rest of the physical archive (e.g. bones, carbonised plant remains, etc.) and do not require specialist archiving. They should be packaged and stored as outlined above (§3.2.1). The general lack of long-term storage for soil and sediment samples means that in some circumstances sub-sampling for cold storage can need to be considered, although this has potential complications for radiocarbon dating of waterlogged plant macrofossils (Wohlfarth et al. 1998).

5 Case studies

5.1 King Alfred Way, Newton Poppleford, Devon

Between October 2014 and October 2017, AC Archaeology undertook archaeological investigations on agricultural land south of King Alfred Way, Newton Poppleford, east of Exeter, Devon (Fig. 31). The work, in response to a planning condition set by East Devon District Council for a residential development on the site, was funded by the developer Cavanna Homes (Rainbird and Lichtenstein 2018).

In 2014 archaeological trench evaluations identified several pits and postholes containing Middle Neolithic pottery, together with buried cultivation soils and large numbers of worked prehistoric flints. Subsequent mitigation in 2017 resulted in the opening of two excavation areas positioned to investigate probable prehistoric features. Following stripping within Area 1, an unsuspected ring ditch with an internal diameter of *c.* 8m was revealed (F1004; Fig. 32a). Sparse finds in the U-shaped ditch — 0.9m–1.5m wide; 0.4–0.6m deep (Fig. 32b) — consisted of 56 pieces of worked flint and a single sherd of later Iron Age pottery. Although no mound, outer or internal bank material, or other features survived in its interior, sections across the ditch showed that its primary fill probably derived from a barrow mound or internal bank that had originally existed.

After the ring ditch had infilled, two stratigraphically-related graves (F1034 and F1041) were dug cutting its inner lip. The earliest of them (F1041) contained the calcined bones of an adult human, a single sherd of Peterborough Ware and

Figure 32: (a) Pre-excavation photograph of Newton Poppleford ring ditch taken using a polecam (© AC Archaeology);
(b) post-excavation photograph of Newton Poppleford ring ditch taken using a polecam (© AC Archaeology).

Laboratory Number	Sample & context	Radiocarbon Age (BP)	$\delta^{13}C_{IRMS}$ (‰)
SUERC-776221F	human bone, calcined, ?mature adult, deposit (1040) from grave F1040	4480±30	−23.1±1.0

Table 5: Radiocarbon and associated stable isotope measurements from Newton Poppleford.

a worked flint. The second grave (F1034) also contained cremated adult human remains, along with three more conjoining ceramic sherds from the same vessel as the sherd from F1041, worked flint, a piece of iron slag, fired clay and two small sherds of later ceramics.

Given that cremation deposits associated with Middle Neolithic ceramics are unexpected and unusual, and the fact that ring ditches of this form would commonly be assigned a Bronze Age date, a radiocarbon determination was obtained from a single fragment of calcined bone from F1041 to determine its age (Table 5)[1]. The result was calibrated with Bchron (Haslett and Parnell 2008) using IntCal20 (Reimer et al. 2020). The calibrated radiocarbon date, 3335–3030 cal BC (95% probability; Fig. 33) provides a *terminus ante quem* for the construction of the ring ditch and is the first example of this monument class in south-west England to have scientific dating.

Although the ring-ditch is a significant archaeological discovery made as a result of the planning process in its own right, radiocarbon dating has situated the monument as belonging to a diverse group of circular earthworks dating the 34–31st centuries cal BC in Britain. Previously the

south-west extent of Neolithic round mounds and ring-ditches in England was believed to be Dorset and Wiltshire (Kinnes 1979; Leary et al. 2010), and so dating of the monument at Newton Poppleford has now extended this distribution into Devon.

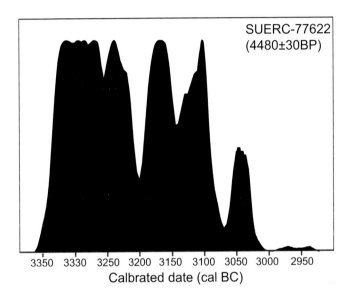

Figure 33: Probability distribution of the date from Newton Poppleford. The distribution is the result of simple radiocarbon calibration (Stuiver and Reimer 1993) (image by P. Marshall).

1. The reported result is a conventional radiocarbon age (Stuiver and Polach 1977). The laboratory maintains a continual programme of quality assurance procedures, in addition to participation in international inter-comparisons (Scott et al. 2017). These tests indicate no laboratory offsets and demonstrate the validity of the precision quoted. The sample dated in SUERC was processed and measured by Accelerator Mass Spectrometry, according to the procedures described in Dunbar et al. (2016).

Figure 34: Map showing location of Greyfriars Leicester (image by P. Marshall).

5.2 The skeleton in the car park

Excavation in 2012 by the University of Leicester on the site of Grey Friars church in Leicester (Fig. 34), demolished after the Reformation and subsequently built over, revealed the remains of the friary church with a grave in a high-status position beneath the choir (Buckley et al. 2013; Fig. 35). The project, to search for the lost grave of King Richard III, the last English king to die in battle, had uncovered a battle-scarred skeleton with spinal curvature. How old are the bones found under the Grey Friars church? Clearly, they cannot be any more recent than the Dissolution of AD 1538. But if they are earlier than AD 1485, then they cannot be the remains of Richard III.

Four samples of rib bone from the individual interred in the grave beneath the choir were dated at the Oxford Radiocarbon Accelerator Unit (ORAU) and Scottish Universities Environmental Research Centre (SUERC). At SUERC the samples were pretreated following a modified Longin (1971) method. They were then combusted to carbon dioxide (Vandeputte et al. 1996), graphitised (Slota et al. 1987), and measured by Accelerator Mass Spectrometry (AMS) (Xu et al. 2004). The samples at ORAU were pretreated and combusted as described in Brock et al. (2010b), graphitised (Dee and Bronk Ramsey 2000) and dated by AMS (Bronk Ramsey et al. 2004a).

Figure 35: The 'skeleton in the car park' *in situ* in his grave shortly after his discovery in 2012 (© University of Leicester Archaeological Services).

Laboratory number	Sample reference & material	Radiocarbon Age (BP)	$\delta^{13}C_{IRMS}$ (‰)	$\delta^{15}N_{IRMS}$ (‰)	C/N
OxA-27182	Greyfriars SK1 sample 1, human bone, rib	478±25	−18.4±0.2	15.0±0.3	
OxA-27183	Greyfriars SK1 sample 2, human bone, rib	480±25	−18.4±0.2	15.3±0.3	
SUERC-42896	Greyfriars 2012 – Burial 1 sample 1, human bone, rib	434±18	−18.7±0.2	14.6±0.3	3.2
SUERC-42897	Greyfriars 2012 – Burial 1 sample 2, human bone, rib	440±17	−18.6±0.2	15.0±0.3	3.2

Table 6: Grey Friars, Leicester radiocarbon and stable isotope results.

The reported conventional radiocarbon ages (Stuiver and Polach 1977) and stable isotope results are shown in Table 6. Both laboratories maintain continual programmes of quality assurance procedures, in addition to participation in international inter-comparisons (Scott et al. 2017). These tests indicate no laboratory offsets and demonstrate the validity of the precision quoted.

The four radiocarbon determinations are statistically consistent at the 5% significance level (T'=3.8; n=3; T'(5%)=7.8; Ward and Wilson 1978) and thus a weighted mean (Grey Friars 2012: 451±11 BP) has been calculated as providing the best estimate for the age of the individual. Calibration of the weighted mean using the probability method (Stuiver and Reimer 1993), and IntCal20 (Reimer et al. 2020) provides a

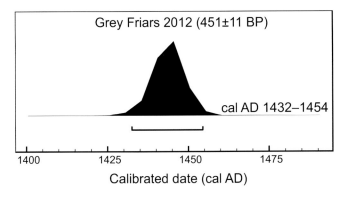

Figure 36: Calibrated radiocarbon date for the Grey Friars 2012 individual, calculated using a fully terrestrial calibration curve (image by P. Marshall).

calibrated date for the death of this person of cal AD 1432–1454 (95% probability; Fig. 36). Clearly taken at face value this would indicate that the remains cannot be those of Richard III, but the stable isotope measurements indicate that this individual had a protein-rich diet that included a significant amount of non-terrestrial food sources. Diet-induced radiocarbon offsets when an individual has taken up carbon from a reservoir not in equilibrium with the terrestrial biosphere can have implications for accurately estimating when a person died.

In order to correct for the dietary information that the stable isotopes provide we need to estimate the contribution of non-terrestrial sources in the diet of the dated individual. A proportional diet profile for the Grey Friars 2012 individual was established using the proportional mixing model FRUITS (Food Reconstruction Using Isotopic Transferred Signals) v 2.1.1 (Fernandes et al. 2014). Baseline isotopic values for food sources used in the FRUITS modelling (Table 7) were drawn from medieval faunal isotope values (Müldner and Richards 2005). As isotopic values for terrestrial vegetation were unavailable, a proxy was derived from the average cattle and sheep isotopic values (Müldner and Richards 2005) less trophic enrichments of 1‰ ($\delta^{13}C$) and 3‰ ($\delta^{15}N$). Human diet-to-consumer enrichment values were set at 4.0±0.5‰ ($\delta^{13}C$; Fernandes 2016) and 5.0±0.5‰ ($\delta^{15}N$; O'Connell et al. 2012), with the weight and concentration of the diet sources comprising 100%, following Fernandes et al. (2014) for unrouted diet models.

Food Source	δ¹³C (‰)	δ¹⁵N (‰)
terrestrial vegetation	−22.8±0.2	2.4±0.2
terrestrial protein	−21.6±0.2	5.9±0.2
eel and freshwater fish	−21.2±0.2	13.7±0.2
marine fish	−13.2±0.2	13.3±0.2

Table 7: Food source isotope values used in the FRUITS analysis. Average isotopic values for the food groups are derived from Müldner and Richards (2005).

Food Source	Estimated diet proportion % (Mean)	SD (%)
terrestrial vegetation	22.4	10.3
terrestrial protein	18.3	14.0
eel and freshwater fish	56.7	6.9
marine fish	2.7	2.3

Table 8: Results for the FRUITS source proportional mixing model for Grey Friars 2012.

The FRUITS source-proportional mixing model (Table 8; Fig. 37) indicates that animal-derived protein contributed 77.6% of the individual's diet. Such protein-rich diets are notable in medieval populations, where meat and fish made up a significant proportion of the food intake for aristocrats, clergy and wealthy merchants (Müldner and Richards 2005, 40). Eel and freshwater fish (56.7±6.9%) account for the greatest proportion of the diet of the individual from Grey Friars, with that from terrestrial protein being considerably smaller (18.3±14%). The contribution from marine fish is estimated to be just 2.7±2.3% of diet, suggesting that diet-derived offsets from marine radiocarbon reservoirs will be minimal; however, the diet derived offsets from eel and freshwater fish could be significant.

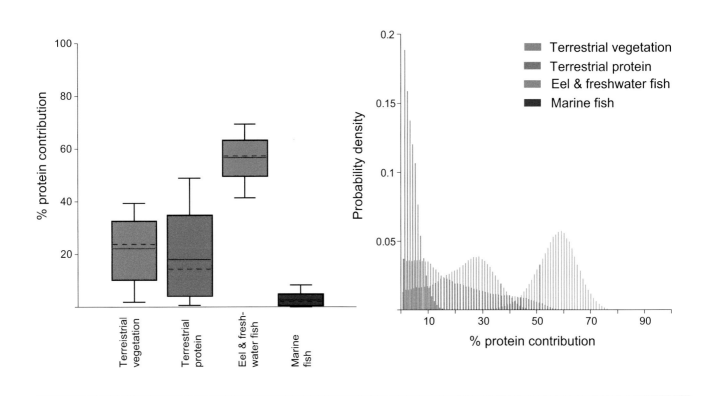

Figure 37: Model outputs from FRUITS analysis of the dietary stable isotope data from the Grey Friars 2012 individual (credible intervals on the left and probability distributions on the right). On the left boxes represent a 68% credible interval (corresponding to the 16th and 84th percentiles), while the whiskers represent a 95% credible interval (corresponding to the 2.5th and 97.5th percentiles). The horizontal dashed lines represent the estimated means, while the horizontal lines represent the estimated medians (50th percentile) (image by P. Marshall).

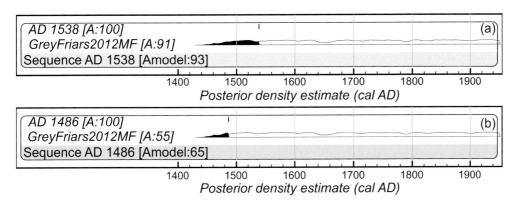

AD 1538 [A:100]
GreyFriars2012MF [A:91]
Sequence AD 1538 [Amodel:93]

(a)

1400   1500   1600   1700   1800   1900
Posterior density estimate (cal AD)

AD 1486 [A:100]
GreyFriars2012MF [A:55]
Sequence AD 1486 [Amodel:65]

(b)

1400   1500   1600   1700   1800   1900
Posterior density estimate (cal AD)

Figure 38: The mixed-source calibration for the Grey Friars 2012 individual, constrained (a) to be earlier than AD 1538 (date of Monastic Dissolution), and (b) to be earlier than AD 1486 (image by P. Marshall).

We can account for the different sources of carbon in the measured radiocarbon age of the individual from Grey Friars by calibrating the result in OxCal 4.4 (Bronk Ramsey 2009a), using a mixture of the terrestrial calibration curve (Reimer et al. 2020), the marine calibration curve (Heaton et al. 2020) with a ΔR correction of −169±56 BP (Harkness 1983) and the terrestrial calibration curve offset for an appropriate freshwater reservoir in the proportions suggested by the dietary analysis (Fig. 37). Given the lack of all-embracing research on freshwater offsets in England, we have implemented a uniform ΔR distribution from 750–0 BP based on the range of offset in archaeological fish bone from Coppergate, Earith and Flixborough (2±54 BP to 703±32 BP) identified by Keaveney and Reimer (2012, table 1). The calibration is constrained by including the prior information that the individual must have been interred before AD 1538.

This suggests that the individual excavated from Grey Friars died in *cal AD 1459–1539 (95% probability; Fig. 38a)*. Furthermore, constraining the death of the individual to be before AD 1486 shows good agreement (Amodel: 65; Fig. 38b). The very wide calibrated date shown in outline in these graphs reflects the great uncertainty on the freshwater reservoir correction, which in this case can be constrained by the historical evidence.

A perfect mitochondrial DNA match was found between the sequence obtained from the Grey Friars skeleton and one living relative of Richard III, and a single-base substitution was found when compared with a second relative. However, Y-chromosome haplotypes from male-line relatives and the Grey Friars skeleton do not match, which could be attributed to a false paternity event

occurring in any of the intervening generations (King et al. 2014). Combining all the non-genetic data (radiocarbon, estimated age at death, sex, presence of scoliosis and presence of perimortem wounds) together with the genetic data (mtDNA and Y-chromosome) in a Bayesian framework, however, does provide extremely strong support for the probability that the skeleton in the car park is that of King Richard III (King et al. 2014; Fig. 39).

Figure 39: King Richard III, *c.* AD 1510–40 (oil on wooden panel) (Society of Antiquaries, Bridgeman Images).

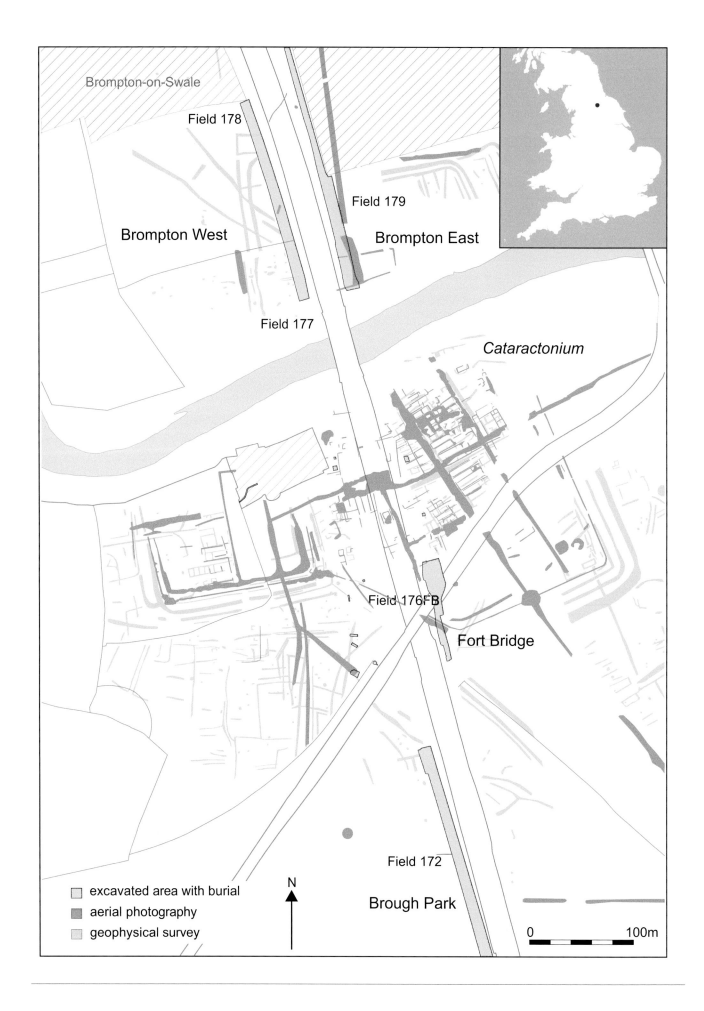

Figure 40: Location of *Cataractonium*, showing the excavated areas, plotting from aerial photography and geophysical survey interpretation (adapted from Speed and Holst (2018, fig 4.2)).

5.3 A slice across *Cataractonium* Roman town

The Leeming to Barton A1 road scheme comprised 19km of road improvements to upgrade the existing dual carriageway to motorway status. Upgrading of the A1 in this part of North Yorkshire passed through an area of known prehistoric and historic significance, including the scheduled Roman town of *Cataractonium*. The aim of the archaeological investigations, undertaken by Northern Archaeological Associates and funded by Highways England, was to mitigate for the impact of road construction works on the extant archaeological remains.

The quantity and quality of the evidence for Roman period activity was exceptional and, in recognition of this, a number of research themes were formulated as part of post-excavation programme, including one focussing on death, burial and identity (Speed and Holst 2018).

At the Roman settlement of *Cataractonium* (Fig. 40), excavations at Brough Park (Field 172), Fort Bridge (Field 176FB), Brompton West (Fields 177/178) and Brompton East (Field 179) recovered 26 inhumations (Fig. 41) and nine cremation burials, including a *bustum* burial that formed part of a small cremation cemetery located at Brough Park (Field 172). At Brompton West (Fields 177/178) a larger number of burials was recorded to the rear of the northern suburb of *Cataractonium*.

In order to understand the chronology of burials at Roman *Cataractonium* and how burials here related to other burials excavated during the road scheme and to Roman burial practices elsewhere, particularly in the north of England, an extensive radiocarbon dating programme was undertaken (Table 9). The samples dated at SUERC were processed and measured by Accelerator Mass Spectrometry, according to the procedures described in Dunbar et al. (2016). The reported results are conventional radiocarbon ages (Stuiver and Polach 1977). The laboratory maintains a continual programme of quality assurance procedures, in addition to participation in international inter-comparisons (Scott 2017). These tests indicate no laboratory offsets and demonstrate the validity of the precision quoted.

When we calibrate a radiocarbon measurement (Fig. 42 – outline distribution), we assume that the calendar date of the sample is equally likely to fall at any point on the calibration curve. For one sample, this is a reasonable assumption; but as soon as we wish to calibrate a second measurement from a site, this assumption is no longer valid. The radiocarbon measurements on burials from *Cataractonium* Roman Town are therefore **related**.

What we need is a way to account for the 'relatedness' of sets of radiocarbon dates. Bayesian statistics enable us to do this. Given that the burials were all found in association with the

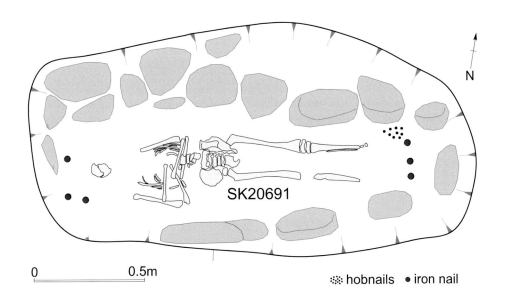

SK20691

0   0.5m

⠿ hobnails   • iron nail

Laboratory code	Sample details	Radiocarbon Age (BP)	$\delta^{13}C_{IRMS}$ (‰)	$\delta^{15}N_{IRMS}$ (‰)	C:N
Field 172 (Brough Park)					
SUERC-75335	human bone, calcined long bone fragments, Grave 6723	1772±34	−19.4±0.2	-	-
SUERC-75336	human bone, calcined femur shaft fragments, Grave 6729	1789±34	−15.5±0.2	-	-
SUERC-75337	human bone, calcined long bone fragments, Grave 6783	1888±34	−19.1±0.2	-	-
SUERC-75334	human bone, calcined tibia shaft, Grave 6785	1817±34	−20±0.2	-	-
Field 176FB (Fort Bridge)					
SUERC-75374	human bone, calcined femur shaft, Grave 18207	1869±34	−25±0.2	-	-
SUERC-77042	human bone, foetus, 24–26 weeks *in utero*, Grave 21162, SK21155	1878±25	−20.3±0.2	8.4±0.3	3.2
SUERC-77043	human bone, perinate, 40 weeks *in utero* to 1 month, Grave 21904, SK21901	1864±25	−19.3±0.2	12.2±0.3	3.2
Field 177 (Brompton West)					
SUERC-76349	human bone, 1–12 years, Grave 1225, SK1223	1752±30	−20.9±0.2	11.3±0.3	3.3
SUERC-75346	human bone, male, 36–45 years, left ulna distal shaft, Grave 20571, SK20573	1745±34	−20.1±0.2	11.3±0.3	3.3
SUERC-75338	human bone, 18+ years, left femur fragment, Grave 20606, SK20604	1763±34	−19.9±0.2	11.0±0.3	3.2
SUERC-75349	human bone, ?female, 18+ years, right tibia fragment, Grave 20616, SK20615	1741±34	−20.5±0.2	10.4±0.3	3.2
SUERC-75339	human bone, 7–12 years, rib fragment, Grave 20621, SK20691	1818±34	−18.7±0.2	11.2±0.3	3.2
SUERC-75347	human bone, ?male, 46+ years, right humerus fragment, Grave 20662, SK20721	1741±34	−19.9±0.2	11.3±0.3	3.2
SUERC-75343	human bone, 36–45 years, left fibula fragment, Grave 20812, SK20813	1712±34	−20.3±0.2	10.4±0.3	3.2
SUERC-75348	human bone, right rib, ?male, 26–35 years, Grave 20796, SK20844	1739±34	−19.9±0.2	10.6±0.3	3.1
SUERC-75345	human bone, male, 36–45 years, left rib fragment, Grave 20955, SK20957	1836±34	−20.4±0.2	10.6±0.3	3.2
SUERC-75344	human bone, ?male, 18+ years, left rib, Grave 20960, SK20962	1774±34	−19.9±0.2	10.2±0.3	3.2

Table 9: This page and opposite.
Cataractonium: radiocarbon and stable isotope measurements.

Roman settlement, we can postulate that when burial started at *Cataractonium*, it continued at a relatively constantly rate for some period of time, and it then ended.

By using the archaeological information that the dates relate to burial activity that continued for a certain period (and that burial started before it ended!), our model can assess how much of the scatter on the radiocarbon dates comes from statistics and how much is real, historical duration. Furthermore, the model formally estimates when burial began and when it ended (*see* §2.1 and §2.2).

The model, implemented in OxCal 4.4 (Bronk Ramsey 2009a; 2017) using IntCal20 (Reimer et al. 2020),is based on the assumption of a uniform rate of burial within and around *Cataractonium* during its occupation (Zeidler et al. 1998). Given that the stable isotope results (Table 9) indicate that the dated individuals consumed a diet predominantly based on terrestrial C3 foods (Fig. 22), the radiocarbon results are unlikely to be affected by any significant reservoir effects, so a fully terrestrial calibration curve can be employed. The model provides estimates for the beginning of burial in *cal AD 160–230* (*95% probability; StartBurial;* Fig. 42), probably in *cal AD 185–220 (68% probability);* and its demise in *cal AD 275–395* (95% probability; *EndBurial;* Fig. 42), probably in *cal AD 315–375 (68% probability)*. Figure 43 shows

Laboratory code	Sample details	Radiocarbon Age (BP)	$\delta^{13}C_{IRMS}$ (‰)	$\delta^{15}N_{IRMS}$ (‰)	C:N
Field 178 (Brompton West)					
SUERC-75354	human bone, calcined femur shaft, Grave 20400	1863±34	−16.1±0.2	-	-
SUERC-75358	human bone, male, 46+ years, right rib, Grave 20114, SK20116	1758±34	−20.3±0.2	10.5±0.3	3.1
SUERC-75364	human bone, female, 26–35 years, left tibia fragment, Grave 20114, SK20117	1742±34	−20.4±0.2	10.8±0.3	3.4
SUERC-75368	human bone, 1–6 years, left femur fragment, Grave 20114, SK20118	1719±34	−20.8±0.2	10.5±0.3	3.3
SUERC-76675	human bone, 1–6 years, Grave 20114, SK20119	1715±32	−19.9±0.2	13.7±0.3	3.3
SUERC-75367	human bone, 1–6 years, rib fragments, Grave 20114, SK20120	1707±34	−20.5±0.2	13.1±0.3	3.2
SUERC-76674	human bone, neonate, birth to 1 month, Grave 21026, SK20188	1811±32	−19.1±0.2	12.4±0.3	3.4
SUERC-75363	human bone, 18+ years, left tibia fragment, Grave 20159, SK20190	1799±34	−19.4±0.2	11.3±0.3	3.3
SUERC-75357	human bone, female, 18+ years, right femur shaft, Grave 20198, SK20197	1784±34	−20.3±0.2	10.3±0.3	3.1
SUERC-75416	human bone, female, 18-25 years, left ulna fragment, Grave 20340, SK20342	1765±30	−19.2±0.2	11.3±0.3	3.2
SUERC-75353	human bone, male, 18-25 years, left fibula fragment, Grave 20418, SK20395	1684±34	−20.6±0.2	10.0±0.3	3.3
SUERC-75356	human bone, male, 36–45 years, left rib, Grave 20417, SK20416	1737±34	−20.3±0.2	9.5±0.3	3.2
SUERC-75359	human bone, ?female, 18+ years, right femur fragment, Grave 20474, SK20475	1754±34	−19.6±0.2	11.9±0.3	3.3
SUERC-75365	human bone, 13-17 years, left tibia fragment, Grave 20476, SK20477	1765±34	−19.6±0.2	10.6±0.3	3.2
SUERC-76673	human bone, perinate, birth to 1 month, Grave 20532, SK20543	1717±32	−19.2±0.2	12.6±0.3	3.4
SUERC-75355	human bone, female, 26–35 years, left tibia fragment, Grave 20532, SK20585	1780±34	−19.8±0.2	10.5±0.3	3.2
SUERC-76672	human bone, 18–25 years, right tibia fragment, Grave 20601, SK20603	1748±32	−20.4±0.2	10.5±0.3	3.3
Field 179 (Brompton East)					
SUERC-75052	human bone, neonate, birth to 1 month, skull fragment, Grave 9343, SK9091	1866±33	−18.1±0.2	12.1±0.3	3.3

the estimated length of the phase of burial activity around *Cataractonium* to be between *50–210 years (95% probability; DurationBurial)*, probably between *95–180 years (68% probability)*.

The dates of the first and last dated burials at Brough Park, Fort Bridge, Brompton West, together with the single dated inhumation from Brompton East are summarised in Figure 44. By comparing the posterior density estimates, it is possible to calculate the probable order of pairs of different events (Table 10). For example, it is *68.5% probable* that the first dated burial at Fort Bridge (*FirstFortBridge*; Fig. 44) began before the first dated burial at Brough Park (*FirstBroughPark*; Fig. 44).

A greater understanding of the chronology of burial practices at Roman *Cataractonium* has provided further insights into how these individual lived their lives and identified themselves within society (Speed and Holst 2018, 599). When integrated with evidence for funerary rites, grave form and accompanying grave goods the chronology has been able to provide glimpses into the spatial variations of society with *Cataractonium*.

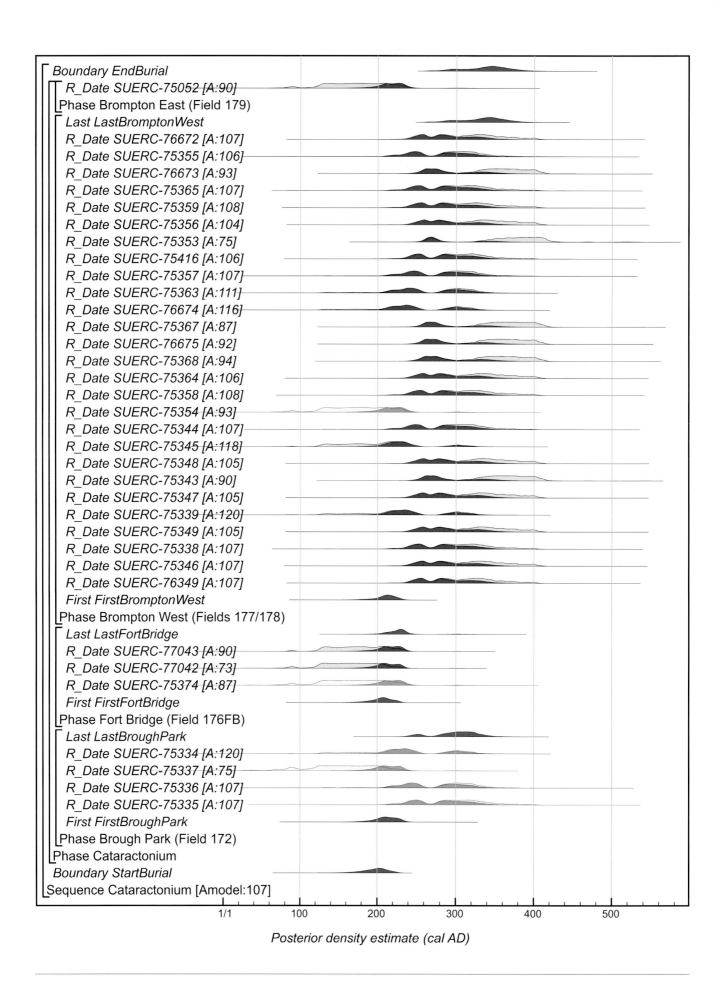

Figure 42: Probability distributions of dates from *Cataractonium*. The format is as in Figure 9 (inhumations are in grey, cremations in red). The large square brackets down the left-hand side of the diagram and the OxCal keywords define the overall model exactly (image by P. Marshall).

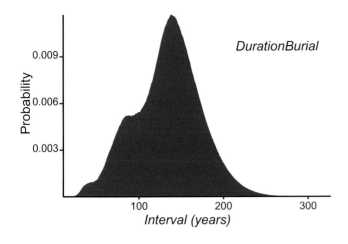

DurationBurial

Figure 43: Probability distribution of the number of years during which burials (inhumation and cremation) were made at *Cataractonium* (derived from the model shown in Figure 42) (image by P. Marshall).

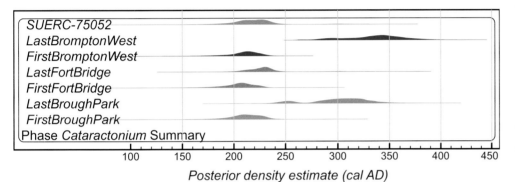

Figure 44: Probability distributions for the beginning and end of burial in different areas of *Cataractonium* (derived from the model shown in Figure 42) (image by P. Marshall).

	First Brough Park	Last Brough Park	First Fort Bridge	Last Fort Bridge	First Brompton West	Last Brompton West	SUERC -75052
FirstBroughPark		100.0	31.5	83.3	46.3	100.0	63.7
LastBroughPark	0.0		0.0	2.4	0.0	94.4	1.8
FirstFortBridge	68.5	100.0		100.0	65.6	100.0	79.2
LastFortBridge	16.7	97.6	0.0		12.9	99.8	31.3
FirstBromptonWest	53.7	100.0	34.4	87.1		100.0	67.2
LastBromptonWest	0.0	5.6	0.0	0.2	0.0		0.1
SUERC-75052	36.4	98.2	20.8	68.7	32.8	99.9	

Table 10: Percentage probabilities of the relative order of first and last dated burials, from the model defined in Figure 42. The cells show the probability of the distribution on the left-hand column being earlier than the distribution on the top row. For example, the probability that *FirstBroughPark* is earlier than *FirstFortBridge* is *31.5%*.

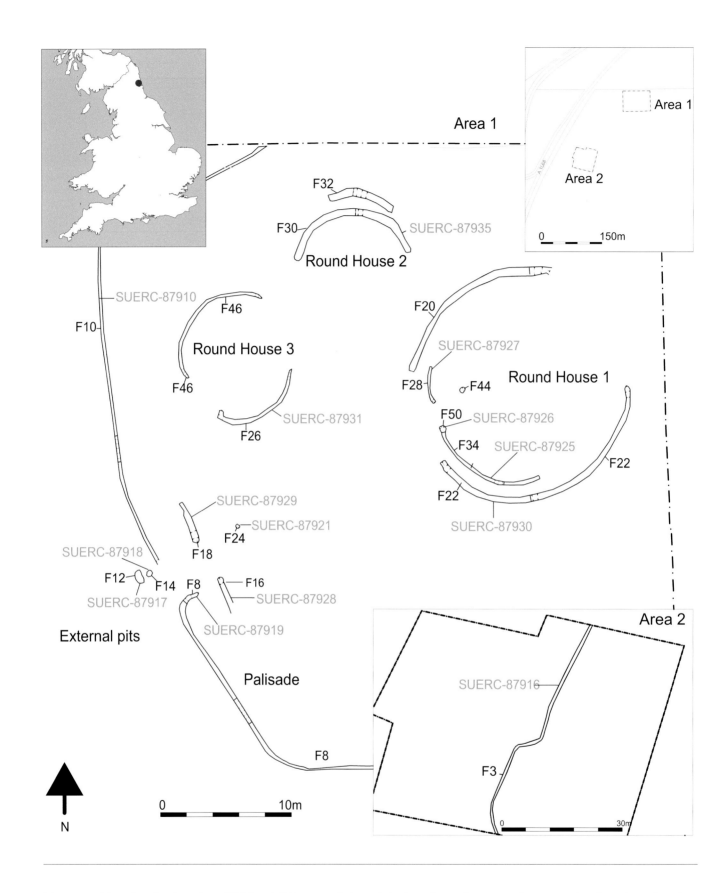

Figure 45: Map showing location of White Hall Farm, and plan of the locations of excavated areas and radiocarbon dated features, adapted from ASDU (2019, figs 4–5) (image by P. Marshall).

Figure 46: Excavated Area 1 at White House Farm showing the sectioned ring gully (F16 and F46) of Round House 3 (© Archaeological Services Durham University).

5.4 An enclosed landscape: Iron Age settlement on the Northumberland plain

Archaeological excavations conducted in advance of housing development at White Hall Farm, Cramlington, Northumberland (Fig. 45) were commissioned by Persimmon Homes and Belway, and undertaken by Archaeological Services Durham University, following an evaluation that identified features together with material culture indicating the presence of an Iron Age settlement and a small ditch of unknown date (ASDU 2019). Two areas were opened for excavation (Areas 1 and 2; Fig. 45), given the potential the site had to contribute to a number of themes in the North East regional research framework (NERRRHE 2022)— in particular: La2 *'How can we improve our understanding of the chronology of late Bronze Age and Iron Age north-east England?';* and La1 *'How can we improve our understanding of late prehistoric settlement and settlement patterns?'.*

Area 1 contained part of a rectilinear settlement enclosed by a palisade within which evidence survived for a central roundhouse (RH1) and two smaller roundhouses (RH2 and RH3; Fig. 46). These structures contained elements of internal wall construction slots together with eaves-drip gullies, and all three appeared to not have been rebuilt. Outside the entrance to the palisaded enclosure, two pits, one probably an open hearth and the other a covered earth oven, represent evidence for earlier activity. Area 2 included part of a ditch.

A total of 14 radiocarbon measurements were made on 14 samples, all but one from Area 1 (Table 11). The samples were processed and measured by Accelerator Mass Spectrometry at SUERC, according to the procedures described in Dunbar et al. (2016). All results are conventional radiocarbon ages (Stuiver and Polach 1977). The laboratory maintains a continual programme of quality assurance procedures, in addition to participation in international inter-comparisons

Laboratory code	Material and context	δ¹³C$_{IRMS}$ (‰)	Radiocarbon Age (BP)
Area1			
SUERC-87917	charcoal: *Corylus avellana*, from the burnt orange-red and brown clay fill [11] of ?open hearth F12	−25.6±0.2	2452±30
SUERC-87918	carbonised nutshell: *Corylus avellana*, from the black sandy silty clay fill [13] of ?earth oven F14	−25.5±0.2	2428±30
SUERC-87919	charcoal: *Alnus glutinosa*, from the fill [7] of the south gully terminus of the palisade F8	−27.1±0.2	2445±30
SUERC-87920	charcoal: *Ilex aquifolium*, from the orange-grey sand fill [15] of the southern ring-gully F22 that formed Round House 1	−24.0±0.2	2287±30
SUERC-87921	charcoal: *Corylus avellana*, from the grey mottled clay fill [23] of posthole F24	−27.0±0.2	2238±30
SUERC-87925	charcoal: *Quercus* sp., from the mottled yellow-grey sandy clay [33] that filled the construction trench F34 for Round House 1	−25.3±0.2	3285±30
SUERC-87926	carbonised nutshell: *Corylus avellana*, from the grey-brown clay fill [49] of posthole F50 in the southern terminal to the entrance of Round House 1	−25.3±0.2	2265±30
SUERC-87927	charcoal: *Betula* sp., from the fill [27] of the construction trench F28 for Round House 1	−23.8±0.2	2187±30
SUERC-87928	charcoal: *Betula* sp., from the grey sandy silty clay [15] that filled F16 an internal construction trench parallel with the palisade	−23.9±0.2	2241±30
SUERC-87929	carbonised nutshell: *Corylus avellana*, from the brown clay loam [17] that filled F18 an internal construction trench parallel with the palisade	−24.9±0.2	2141±30
SUERC-87930	charcoal: *Betula* sp., from the fill [9] of palisade trench F10	−27.3±0.2	2193±30
SUERC-87931	charcoal: *Alnus glutinosa*, from the fill [25] of the southern of penannular ring ditch F26 that formed Round House 3	−26.9±0.2	2185±30
SUERC-87935	charcoal: *Ilex aquifolium*, from the mottled yellow grey-clay fill [29] of the inner gully F30 that formed Round House 2	−23.2±0.2	2179±30
Area 2			
SUERC-87916	charcoal: *Quercus* sp., from the secondary fill [5] of F3 a 0.5m wide, 0.25m deep linear ditch	−25.6±0.2	2212±30

Table 11: White Hall Farm, Northumberland: radiocarbon and stable isotope measurements.

(Scott et al. 2017). These tests indicate no laboratory offsets and demonstrate the validity of the precision quoted.

Eleven samples were single fragments of charcoal, and the remaining three were single fragments of hazelnut shell. All the charcoal fragments were identified as from relatively short-lived species, bar two that were from oak of unknown maturity (SUERC-87916 and SUERC-87925). From Area 1 the samples from F12 (SUERC-87917) and F14 (SUERC-87918) derive from primary fuel debris deposits associated with the use of the pits dug before the construction of the palisaded enclosure settlement (§3.2.2). The remaining 11 samples

from Area 1 derived from postholes, gullies and trenches related to the construction and use of the roundhouses, and from the primary fill of the palisade trench. These 11 samples therefore most likely derived from activity associated with the construction and use of the settlement, although SUERC-87925, from the fill of the construction trench F34 for Round House 1, is clearly residual; and the fragment of charcoal (SUERC-87919) from the fill of F8 appears to be associated with the use of the external pits. The samples from the two external pits have been interpreted as freshly deposited in their contexts, and those from the palisaded enclosure settlement as deriving from its use, apart from SUERC-87919 and SUERC-87925, which have been modelled as *termini post quem* using the AFTER function in OxCal (shown in Fig. 47).

The model for this case study has been calculated in OxCal v4.4 (Bronk Ramsey 2009a) using IntCal20 (Reimer et al. 2020), includes the archaeological interpretation that the dated material from the Area 1 palisaded enclosure settlement derives from a single continuous phase of activity (Buck et al. 1992) and that its relationship to the other dated material from the external pits outside its entrance and from Area 2 is unknown.

The model has good overall agreement (Amodel: 93; Fig. 47) and suggests that the enclosed rectilinear settlement was established in *430–220 cal BC (95% probability; startRectilinearSettlement; Fig. 47)* probably *405–300 cal BC (68% probability)* and ended in *345–120 cal BC (95% probability; endRectilinearSettlement; Fig. 47)* probably *280–160 cal BC (68% probability)*. By comparing the estimated dates for start and end of activity associated with the enclosed rectilinear settlement, we can suggest that it was in use for *1–200 years (95% probability; RectilinearSettlement Fig. 48)*, probably for *30–135 years (68% probability)*.

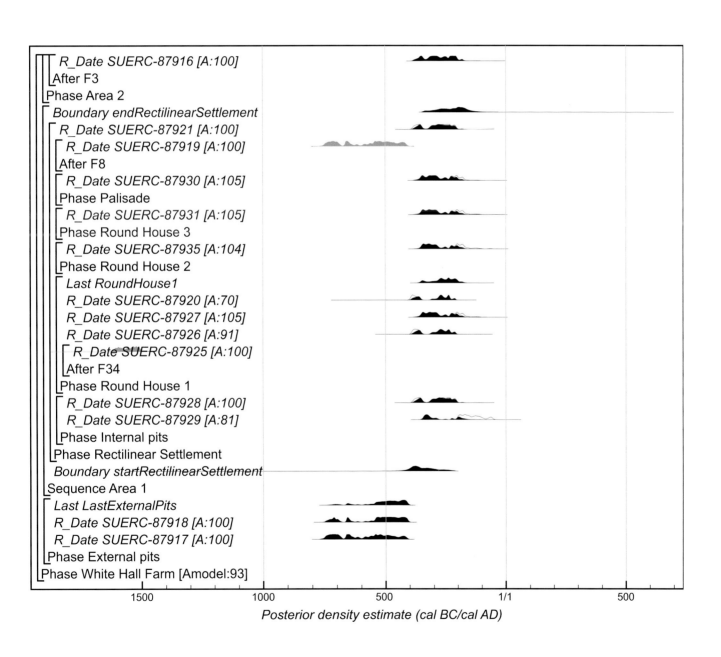

Figure 47: Probability distributions of dates from White Hall Farm. The format is as in Figure 9. The large square brackets down the left-hand side of the diagram and the OxCal keywords define the overall model exactly (image by P. Marshall).

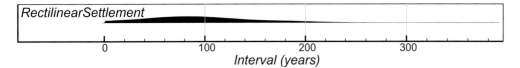

Figure 48: Probability distribution of the number of years the enclosed rectilinear settlement at White Hall Farm was in use, derived from the model shown in Figure 47 (image by P. Marshall).

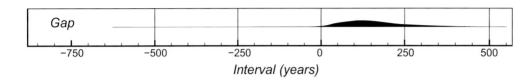

Figure 49: Probability distribution of the number of years between the two pits outside the enclosure entrance at White Hall Farm and the beginning of activity associated with the enclosed rectilinear settlement, derived from the model shown in Figure 47 (image by P. Marshall).

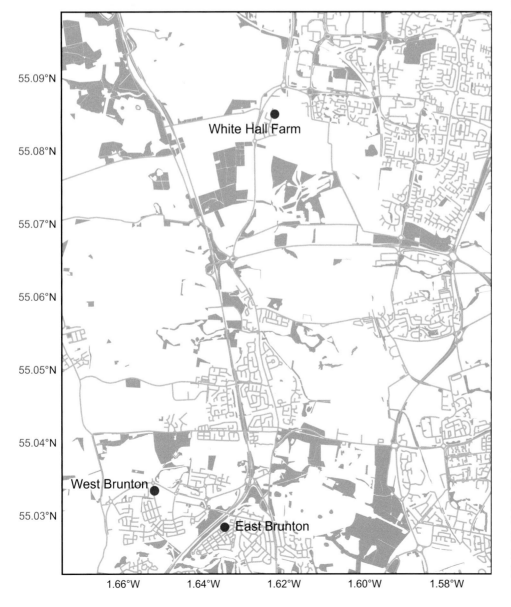

Figure 50: Map of the Northumberland coastal plain showing the location of the White Hall Farm, East Brunton and West Brunton settlements (image by P. Marshall).

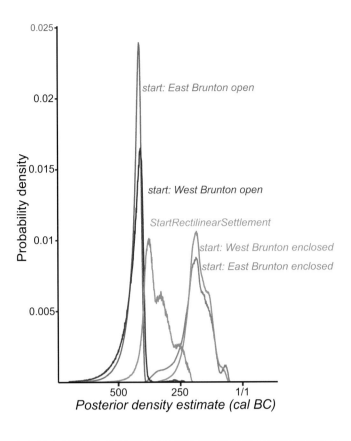

start: East Brunton open

start: West Brunton open

StartRectilinearSettlement

start: West Brunton enclosed

start: East Brunton enclosed

Figure 51: Probability distributions for the beginning of settlement at White Hall Farm, East Brunton and West Brunton. The distributions are derived from Figure 47 and from models defined in Hamilton (2010, figs 6.2.3 (East Brunton) and 6.3.3 (West Brunton)) recalculated using IntCal20 (image by P. Marshall).

The food preparation activity represented by the two pits outside the enclosure entrance predates the beginning of activity associated with the enclosed rectilinear settlement by *1–370 years (95% probability; Gap; Fig. 49) probably 40–215 years (68% probability)*. This interval has been calculated as the difference between the estimated last dated material associated with the external pits *(LastExternalPits)* and the estimated start of activity associated with the enclosed rectilinear settlement *(startRectilinearSettlement)*.

The secondary fill of the ditch in Area 2 was deposited sometime in the late Iron Age and it is therefore plausible that it relates to wider use of the landscape by the inhabitants of the enclosed rectilinear settlement.

This dating of the enclosed rectilinear settlement at White Hall Farm is further evidence for the

start of more permanent settlement in the area and a landscape that became increasingly 'enclosed' on the Northumberland coastal plain in the third quarter of the 1st millennium cal BC. Previous dating of nearby sites of East and West Brunton (Hamilton 2010; Fig. 50) demonstrates that it is *87% probable* that the beginning of activity associated with the enclosed rectilinear settlement at White Hall Farm post-dates the start of unenclosed settlement at East and West Brunton, but predates their 'enclosure' (Fig. 51).

Figure 52: Map showing location of Woolwich, Greater London (image by P. Marshall).

5.5 Geoarchaeological investigations at 2 Pier Road, North Woolwich, London

Increasing redevelopment of the former industrial parts of east London, and the infringement of urban sprawl into parts of Essex and Kent driven by the growing requirements of the city, has resulted in a major expansion in developer-funded archaeological work over the last decade (Fig. 52). Geoarchaeological investigations in advance of residential and commercial development at 2 Pier Road, North Woolwich, London Borough of Newham (Fig. 53), undertaken by Museum of London Archaeology (MoLA) and funded by Higgins Construction Plc, led to the recovery of alluvial sequences that contained an archive of Holocene environmental change, and in particular of changes in relative sea level and regional vegetation cover (Stastney et al. 2021).

In order to provide a chronological framework for the multi-proxy environmental work undertaken on core BH03 from 2 Pier Road, seven AMS radiocarbon dates were obtained (Table 12). The three samples dated at SUERC were processed and measured by Accelerator Mass Spectrometry,

Figure 53: View across the Thames from Woolwich to the North Woolwich Pier terminal, with 2 Pier Road on the right (© Historic England Archive).

according to the procedures described in Dunbar et al. (2016) and those at Beta Analytic were dated by AMS following the methods outlined at https://www.radiocarbon.com/. The reported results are conventional radiocarbon ages (Stuiver and Polach 1977). Both laboratories maintain continual programmes of quality assurance procedures, in addition to participation in international inter-

comparisons (Scott et al. 2017). These tests indicate no laboratory offsets and demonstrate the validity of the precision quoted.

These dates have been included in the age-depth model shown in Figure 54, constructed using rBacon (https://cran.r-project.org/web/packages/rbacon/index.html) and the IntCal20 terrestrial

Laboratory code	Sample material and context	$\delta^{13}C_{IRMS}$ (‰)	Radiocarbon Age (BP)
Beta-515736	carbonised *Triticum spelta* grain from 5.81m b.g.l. (−1.03m OD)	−22.2±0.2	1860±30
Beta-535960	waterlogged, *Alnus* catkin from 5.94m b.g.l. (−1.16m OD)	−25.9±0.2	3020±30
Beta-535961	waterlogged, *Alnus* catkin from 6.35m b.g.l. (−1.57m OD)	−28.0±0.2	3140±30
SUERC-88162	waterlogged, *Alnus* catkin from 7.21m b.g.l. (−2.43m OD)	−25.7±0.2	4136±30
SUERC-88163	waterlogged, *Alnus* catkin from 7.78m b.g.l. (−3.00m OD)	−25.0±0.2	5019±30
Beta-515737	waterlogged, *Alnus* catkin from 8.47m b.g.l. (−3.69m OD)	−26.5±0.2	5019±30
SUERC-88164	waterlogged, *Alnus* catkin from 8.85m b.g.l. (−4.07m OD)	−25.0±0.2	5506±30

Table 12: Radiocarbon and associated stable isotope measurements from 2 Pier Road, North Woolwich, London.

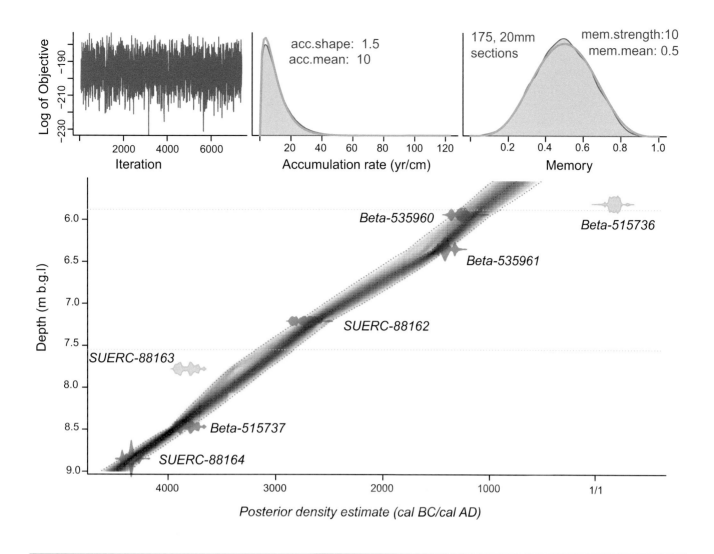

Figure 54: Age-depth model constructed using rBacon (https://cran.r-project.org/web/packages/rbacon/index.html) from core BH03, 2 Pier Road, North Woolwich. The 95% highest posterior density regions (grey) indicate the uncertainty of the ages assigned to the samples between the dated depths. The probability distributions represent the calibrated radiocarbon dates, with those in pink excluded by the model (image by P. Marshall).

dataset for the northern hemisphere (Reimer et al. 2020). Given the evidence that different litho-facies formed under different depositional environments (Stastney et al. 2021, table 1), we have included boundaries at 7.55m b.g.l. (channel margin/semi-terrestrial alder carr) and 5.88m b.g.l. (semi terrestrial alder carr/intertidal floodplain) to take account for potential changes in accumulation rates.

Age-depth modelling implemented with rBacon is similar to that outlined in Blaauw and Christen (2005), but more numerous and shorter sections are used to generate a more flexible chronology

(Blaauw and Christen 2011). Radiocarbon age distributions are derived from the Student-t distribution, which produces calibrated distributions with longer tails than the Normal model (Christen and Pérez 2009). The longer tails on radiocarbon dates, and a prior assumption of unidirectional sediment accumulation, mean that in most cases excluding outliers is not necessary when using rBacon.

The memory or coherence in accumulation rates through a sequence is a parameter based on the degree to which the accumulation rate at each interval depends on the previous interval. Thus, the memory for modelling accumulation in

Palaeoenvironmental event	Position (depth – m b.g.l) & elevation (m OD)	Highest Posterior Density interval (95% probability)
Ulmus decline	8.64m b.g.l. (−3.86m OD)	*4210–3980 cal BC*
1st appearance of cereal pollen	7.70m b.g.l. (−2.92m OD)	*3345–2980 cal BC*
start of peat formation	7.55m b.g.l. (−2.77m OD)	*3185–2830 cal BC*
Tilia decline	6.40m b.g.l. (−1.62m OD)	*1835–1450 cal BC*

Table 13: Highest Posterior Density intervals for the dates of key palaeoenvironmental events at 2 Pier Road, North Woolwich, London, derived from the model shown in Figure 54.

organic-rich (peat) sediments is higher than for lacustrine sediments because accumulation of peat in peat bogs is less dynamic over time than the accumulation of sediments in a lake. We used the default memory properties given in Blaauw and Christen (2011; mem.strength = 4 and mem. mean = 0.7).

The treatment of outliers in rBacon is analogous to the OxCal General Outlier Model (Bronk Ramsey 2009b) in that both draw from a long-tailed Student-t distribution. The number of parameters employed in the process by rBacon is significantly different from OxCal, generally resulting in more flexibility towards potential outliers than the approach implemented in

OxCal, and also enabling the model to account for possible unknown or underestimated errors associated with the ^{14}C determinations (Christen and Pérez 2009).

The resulting age-depth model is shown in Figure 54 along with plots that describe: (top left panel) the stability of the model (log objective vs iteration); (top middle panel) the prior (entered by the user) and posterior (resulting) accumulation rate, and; (top right panel) the prior and posterior memory properties.

The model has excluded two dates, SUERC-88163 and Beta-515736. The *Alnus* catkin, SUERC-88163, appears to be residual and probably represents

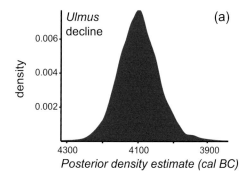

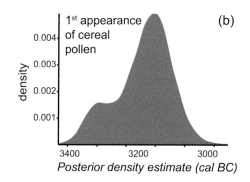

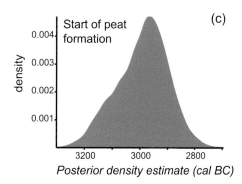

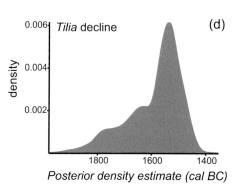

Figure 55: Probability distributions for the estimated date of the *Ulmus* decline (blue), first appearance of cereal pollen (orange), start of peat formation (mauve) and the *Tilia* decline (green) at 2 Pier Road, North Woolwich, core BH03, derived from the model shown in Figure 54 (image by P. Marshall).

reworked material from the river channel margins. The carbonised spelt grain, Beta-515736, would appear to be intrusive (cf Pelling et al. 2015), as it was an isolated find among a plant macrofossil assemblage dominated by species associated with wetlands and marshy ground (Stastney et al. 2021, 5). The wider tails of the rBacon calibration model reduce the need for detecting and removing outliers (Blaauw and Christen (2011, 476). The model is very stable (Fig. 54, top left panel) with the posteriors for the accumulation rate and its variability showing excellent comparability to their priors (Fig. 54, top middle/right panels).

Producing an age-depth model is often the first step towards determining the age of 'events' in proxy records at specific depths in a sequence that are not directly dated. For example, the *Ulmus* decline recorded in the BH03 pollen diagram (Stastney et al. 2021, fig. 5) at 8.64m bgl is estimated to have taken place in *4210–3980 cal BC (95% probability;* Fig. 55a; Table 13) and the *Tilia* decline (6.40m bgl) in *1835–1450 cal BC (95% probability;* Fig. 55d).

Age-depth models have the potential to significantly increase our ability to accurately date past events and thus to better understand past environmental changes and human impact on the landscape, but good prior information is essential for reliable age-depth models, particularly in cases where sequences have low numbers of radiocarbon dates.

Figure 56: Map showing location of Harthill with Woodall, South Yorkshire (image by P. Marshall).

5.6 ¹⁴C wiggle-matching at 4 Walesker Lane, Harthill with Woodall, South Yorkshire

The four-bay house at 4 Walseker Lane, Harthill with Woodall, near Rotherham (Fig. 56), is believed to be one of the earliest domestic buildings so far identified in South Yorkshire (Ryder 1987). The medieval house apparently consisted of a central two-bay hall flanked by end bays. The shorter eastern bay of the hall perhaps housed the dais, with the bay beyond containing the solar, its status suggested by the collar purlin and braces over the bay being neatly chamfered. At the west end of the hall a substantial stone wall and details of the carpentry in the roof above, may suggest the position of the original hearth. The impressive crown-post roof survives virtually intact (Fig. 57).

Tree-ring analysis was commissioned to inform renovations of the building in 2019 (Arnold et al. 2020a). All timbers were from very fast-grown trees and were of clearly marginal suitability for dating by ring-width dendrochronology. A hybrid approach was therefore adopted using dendrochronology and radiocarbon wiggle-matching in partnership. Core samples were obtained on two separate occasions (Table 14). Eight timbers were sampled in April 2019 and, following initial tree-ring analysis, which failed to produce grouping between any of the ring-width series, four single-ring samples from different timbers were submitted for radiocarbon dating to confirm the extent of surviving early fabric in the hall roof. A further eight core samples were obtained in July 2019, which enabled the grouping and tentative dating of the ring-width series. Seven more samples were then submitted for

Figure 57: East–west view of the crown-post roof undergoing repairs at 4 Walseker Lane, Harthill, showing truss 1 in the foreground with truss 2 beyond (photograph by R. Howard).

radiocarbon dating to confirm the tentative dating suggested by the ring-width dendrochronology, and to test further tentative statistical and visual cross-matching between the ring-width series.

The annual growth ring-widths of all but one sample were measured. Allowing for the short lengths of the sample series, these measured data were then compared with each other by the Litton/Zainodin grouping procedure (Litton and Zainodin 1991; Laxton et al. 1988). This resulted in the production of a single cross-matching group of ten samples, which formed at a minimum t-value of 3.7. The ring-width series were combined to form site chronology WLSKSQ01A (Fig. 58), which was compared to the reference chronologies for oak. This indicated that WLSKSQ01A cross-matched

at two different possible positions with similar t-value levels (Table 15a–b), and so cannot be dated by ring-width dendrochronology.

Site chronology WLSKSQ01A was then compared with the five remaining measured but ungrouped samples. This indicated tentative statistical cross-matching with a further three samples, this 13-sample group forming at a minimum t-value of 3.1. These 13 ring-width series were also combined at the offset positions to form site chronology WLSKSQ01B (Fig. 58), which was similarly compared to the reference chronologies with inconclusive results (Table 15a–b).

The two measured samples that remain ungrouped both have less than 30 rings, which is insufficient for even tentative statistical cross-

Sample number	Sample location	Total rings	Sapwood rings	Sapwood rings	Relative date of first measured ring	Relative date of last heartwood ring	Relative date of last heartwood ring
WLS-K01	tiebeam, truss 1	49	8	8	4[SQ01A]	44[SQ01A]	52[SQ01A]
WLS-K02	crown post, truss 1	57	15C	15C	1[SQ01A]	42[SQ01A]	57[SQ01A]
WLS-K02A	ditto	54	15C	15C	4[SQ01A]	42[SQ01A]	57[SQ01A]
WLS-K02B	ditto	57	15C	15C	1[SQ01A]	42[SQ01A]	57[SQ01A]
WLS-K03	south principal rafter, truss 1	35	2	2	13[SQ01A]	45[SQ01A]	47[SQ01A]
WLS-K04	south common rafter 9 (from east), bay 1	40	21C	21C	18[SQ01B]	36[SQ01B]	57[SQ01B]
WLS-K05	north wall plate, truss 1 – 2	10nm	---	---	---	---	---
WLS-K06	tiebeam, truss 2	25	9	9	31[SQ01C]	46[SQ01C]	55[SQ01C]
WLS-K07	brace, south wall post to tiebeam, truss 2	32	h/s	h/s	15[SQ01A]	46[SQ01A]	46[SQ01A]
WLS-K08	crown post, truss 2	28	7	7	24[SQ01C]	44[SQ01C]	51[SQ01C]
WLS-K09	east hip, common rafter 5 (from north)	50	18c	18c	6[SQ01A]	37[SQ01A]	55[SQ01A]
WLS-K10	south common rafter 5, bay 1	38	14C	14C	20[SQ01B]	43[SQ01B]	57[SQ01B]
WLS-K11	south common rafter 10, bay 1	37	16C	16C	21[SQ01A]	41[SQ01A]	57[SQ01A]
WLS-K12	south common rafter 2, bay 3	43	13C	13C	15[SQ01A]	44[SQ01A]	57[SQ01A]
WLS-K13	collar frame 7, bay 3	37	11C	11C	21[SQ01B]	46[SQ01B]	57[SQ01B]
WLS-K14	crown post, truss 3	34	13C	13C	24[SQ01A]	44[SQ01A]	57[SQ01A]
WLS-K15	north outer strut, truss 3	38	10	10	19[SQ01A]	46[SQ01A]	56[SQ01A]
WLS-K16	north common rafter 1, bay 4	45	18C	18C	13[SQ01A]	39[SQ01A]	57[SQ01A]

C = complete sapwood is retained on the sample, the last measured ring date is the felling date of the timber represented

c = complete sapwood is found on the timber, but a portion of this has been lost from the sample in coring

h/s = the heartwood/sapwood ring is the last ring on the sample

nm = sample not measured

[SQ01A] = relative date span within site master chronology WLSKSQ01A (secure statistical cross-matching for ten samples)

[SQ01B] = relative date span within site master chronology WLSKSQ01B (tentative statistical cross-matching for an extra three samples)

[SQ01C] = relative date span within site master chronology WLSKSQ01C (tentative visual cross-matching for an extra two samples)

Table 14: Details of tree-ring samples from 4 Walseker Lane, Harthill with Woodall, Rotherham, South Yorkshire. Tree-ring cores sub-sampled for radiocarbon dating are shown in red.

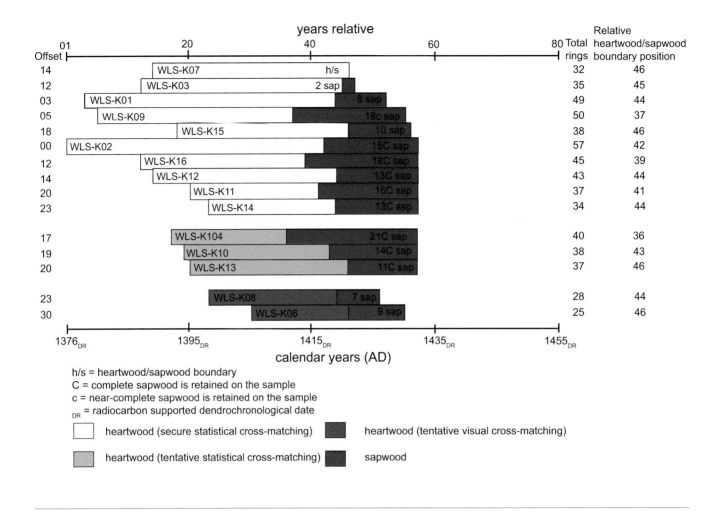

Figure 58: Bar diagram of the samples in site chronology WLSKSQ01C at 4 Walseker Lane, Harthill (adapted from Arnold et al. 2020a, fig. 6c).

matching. However, an attempt was made to cross-match the ring-width series from these two samples visually with the other measured series from this building (Fig. 59). These additional two ring-width series were then combined with the 13 ring-width series included in WLSKSQ01B to form site chronology WLSKSQ01C (Fig. 58), which was again compared to the reference chronologies with inconclusive results (Table 15a–b).

The radiocarbon wiggle-matching was thus needed to confirm the inconclusive dating suggested by ring-width dendrochronology for site master sequences WLSKSQ01A–C, and to validate the tentative cross-matching of additional samples suggested both by weak statistical correlation (WLSKSQ01B) and by visual matching (WLSKSQ01C) (Fig. 59).

A Bayesian approach has been adopted for the radiocarbon wiggle-matching (Christen and Litton 1995), which incorporates the gaps between each dated annual ring in site master sequence WLSKSQ01C (Fig. 60), along with the radiocarbon measurements from all five cores that have been sampled for radiocarbon dating (Table 16)[2]. Two of these are securely linked to this sequence by statistics (WLS-K01 and WLS-K02A), one is tentatively linked to it by statistics (WLS-K04), and two are tentatively linked by visual matching (WLS-K06 and WLS-K08). The model has been calculated using OxCal v4.4 (Bronk Ramsey 2009a) and IntCal20 (Reimer et al. 2020), and has good overall agreement (Acomb: 145.5, An: 21.3, n: 11; Fig. 61).

Reference chronology	Span of chronology	WLSKSQ01A t-value	WLSKSQ01B t-value	WLSKSQ01C t-value	Reference
110/112 Uppergate Road, Sheffield, South Yorkshire	AD 1370–1507	5.7	5.4	5.6	Hillam and Ryder 1980
Pedagogue's House, Stratford upon Avon, Warwickshire	AD 1377–1502	5.4	5.6	---	Arnold and Howard 2006
Stank Hall Barn, Leeds, West Yorkshire	AD 1384–1444	5.2	6.0	5.3	Hillam and Groves 1991
Stockbridge Farm, Arksey, South Yorkshire	AD 1387–1564	5.1	5.1	4.7	Morgan 1980
Headlands Hall, Liversedge, West Yorkshire	AD 1388–1487	5.1	5.4	5.2	Tyers 2001
Peel Hall, Manchester, Greater Manchester	AD 1378–1481	4.9	4.9	4.7	Leggett 1980
Old Rectory, Cossington, Leicestershire	AD 1375–1526	4.5	4.1	3.5	Howard et al. 1992
41-47 High Street, Exeter, Devon	AD 1342–1636	4.5	4.2	3.3	Arnold et al. 2020b
Horbury Hall, Wakefield, West Yorkshire	AD 1368–1473	4.4	4.5	3.5	Howard et al. 1992
23 Church Street, Eckington, Derbyshire	AD 1381–1474	4.3	4.5	5.1	Esling et al. 1989

Table 15a: Results of the ring-width cross-matching of site chronologies WLSKSQ01A, WLSKSQ01B and WLSKSQ01C when the first-ring date is AD 1376 and the last-ring date is AD 1432 (--- = t-value < 3.0).

Reference chronology	Span of chronology	WLSKSQ01A t-value	WLSKSQ01B t-value	WLSKSQ01C t-value	Reference
St Nicholas' Church, Stanford, Northamptonshire	AD 1349–1482	5.5	5.6	5.4	Howard et al. 1996
Dauntsey House, Dauntsey, Wiltshire	AD 1393–1580	5.4	5.2	4.7	Bridge et al. 2014
St John the Baptist Church, Myndtown, Shropshire	AD 1420–1568	5.3	5.3	5.7	Arnold et al. 2022
Brampton Bierlow Hall, Rotherham, South Yorkshire	AD 1423–1536	5.1	5.0	5.0	Hillam 1984
The Old House, Norwell, Nottinghamshire	AD 1340–1494	4.9	4.8	4.7	Hurford et al. 2010
Flores House, Oakham, Rutland	AD 1408–1591	4.9	4.9	5.0	Hurford et al. 2008
Gorcott Hall, Redditch, Warwickshire	AD 1385–1531	4.8	4.9	4.8	Nayling 2006
Hanson Hall barn, Normanton, West Yorkshire	AD 1359–1455	4.6	4.5	3.9	Tyers 2008
Bucknell Barn, Shropshire	AD 1414–1595	4.5	3.9	4.5	Leggett 1980
All Saints Church, Knipton, Leicestershire	AD 1414–1490	4.4	4.8	4.3	Arnold et al. 2005

Table 15b: Results of the ring-with cross-matching of site chronologies WLSKSQ01A, WLSKSQ01B and WLSKSQ01C when the first-ring date is AD 1407 and the last-ring date is AD 1463.

2. Radiocarbon dating was undertaken at ETH Zürich, Switzerland in 2019–20. Cellulose was extracted using the base-acid-base-acid-bleaching (BABAB) method (Němec et al. (2010), combusted and graphitised (Wacker et al. (2010a), and dated by Accelerator Mass Spectrometry (Synal et al. 2007; Wacker et al. 2010b). Data reduction was undertaken as described by Wacker et al. (2010c). The facility maintains a continual programme of quality assurance procedures (Sookdeo et al. 2020), in addition to participation in international inter-comparison exercises (Scott et al. 2017; Wacker et al. 2020). The results are conventional radiocarbon ages, corrected for fractionation using $\delta^{13}C$ values measured by AMS (Stuiver and Polach 1977).

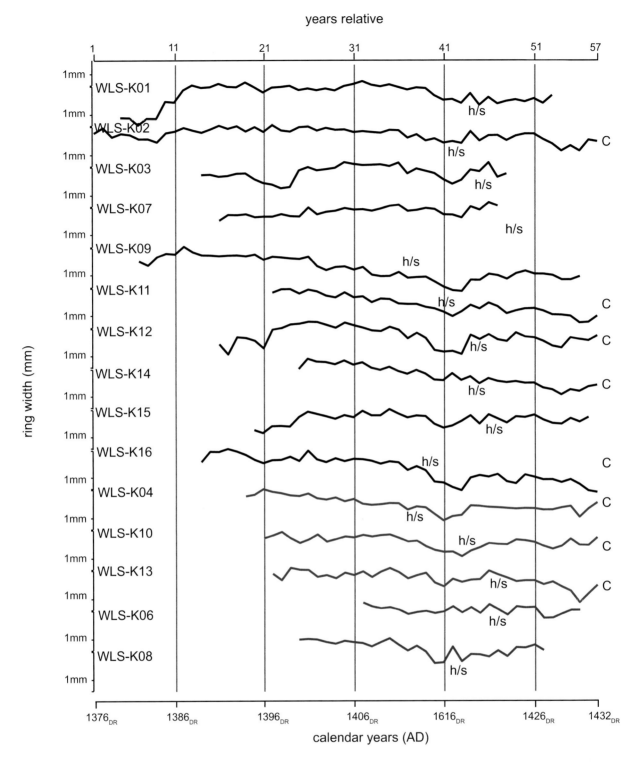

Figure 59: Plots of ring-widths (in mm on a logarithmic scale) of the 15 measured tree-ring series from the hall roof, at 4 Walseker Lane, Harthill (adapted from Arnold et al. 2020a, fig .7).

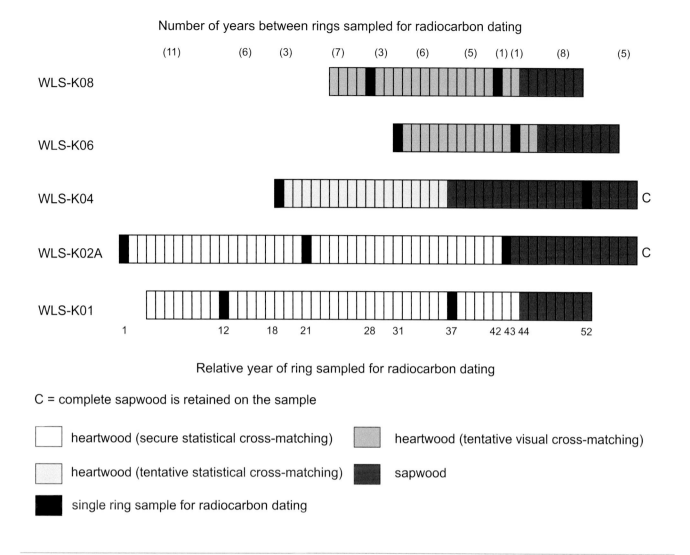

Number of years between rings sampled for radiocarbon dating

(11) (6) (3) (7) (3) (6) (5) (1)(1) (8) (5)

WLS-K08

WLS-K06

WLS-K04   C

WLS-K02A   C

WLS-K01

1   12   18   21   28   31   37   42 43 44   52

Relative year of ring sampled for radiocarbon dating

C = complete sapwood is retained on the sample

☐ heartwood (secure statistical cross-matching)   ▨ heartwood (tentative visual cross-matching)

▨ heartwood (tentative statistical cross-matching)   ▓ sapwood

■ single ring sample for radiocarbon dating

Figure 60: Schematic illustration of samples WLS-K01, WLS-K02A, WLS-K04, WLS-K06, and WLS-K08 to locate the single-ring sub-samples submitted for radiocarbon dating (image by A. Bayliss and P. Marshall).

Laboratory number	Sample	Relative year	Radiocarbon Age (BP)	$\delta^{13}C_{AMS}$ (‰)
ETH-104562	WLS-K01, ring 9 (*Quercus* sp. heartwood)	12[SQ01A]	618±14	−25.9
ETH-99776	WLS-K01, ring 34 (*Quercus* sp. heartwood)	37[SQ01A]	539±13	−23.9
ETH-104563	WLS-K02A, ring 1 (*Quercus* sp. heartwood)	1[SQ01A]	637±14	−25.2
ETH-104564	WLS-K02A, ring 21 (*Quercus* sp. heartwood)	21[SQ01A]	568±14	−25.1
ETH-99777	WLS-K02A, ring 43 (*Quercus* sp. sapwood)	43[SQ01A]	542±13	−22.7
ETH-104565	WLS-K04, ring 1 (*Quercus* sp. heartwood)	18[SQ01B]	575±14	−25.5
ETH-104566	WLS-K04, ring 35 (*Quercus* sp. heartwood)	52[SQ01B]	499±14	−24.5
ETH-104567	WLS-K06, ring 1 (*Quercus* sp. heartwood)	31[SQ01C]	560±14	−24.4
ETH-99778	WLS-K06, ring 14 (*Quercus* sp. heartwood)	44[SQ01C]	517±13	−23.4
ETH-104568	WLS-K08, ring 5 (*Quercus* sp. heartwood)	28[SQ01C]	580±14	−25.6
ETH-99779	WLS-K08, ring 19 (*Quercus* sp. heartwood)	42[SQ01C]	529±13	−24.0

[SQ01A] = relative date within site master chronology WLSKSQ01A (secure statistical cross-matching)
[SQ01B] = relative date within site master chronology WLSKSQ01B (tentative statistical cross-matching)

Table 16: Radiocarbon measurements and associated $\delta^{13}C$ values from oak samples WLS-K01, WLS-K02A, WLS-K04, WLS-K06 and WLS-K08.

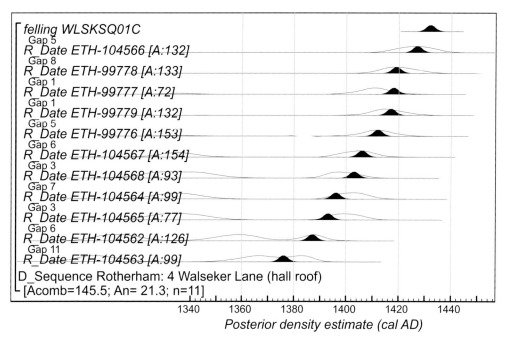

Figure 61: Probability distributions of dates from WLSKSQ01C of roof timbers at 4 Walseker Lane, Harthill. The format is identical to that of Figure 9. The large square brackets down the left-hand side along with the OxCal keywords define the overall model exactly (image by A. Bayliss).

The two radiocarbon dates from core WLS-K04, which is only tentatively linked to the site master on statistical grounds, have good individual agreement in the model (*ETH-104565, A: 76* and *ETH-104566, A:132;* Fig. 61), as do the four radiocarbon dates from cores WLS-K06 and WLS-K08, both of which are only tentatively linked by visual matching to the site master chronology (*ETH-104567*, A: 154, *ETH-99778*, A: 133, *ETH-104568*, A: 93, and *ETH-99779*, A: 133; Fig. 61). These statistics suggest that the offset positions tentatively suggested by the statistical and visual cross-matching of the ring-width data are valid.

The model suggests that the final ring of WLSKSQ01C formed in cal *AD 1428–1436 (95% probability; WLSKSQ01C felling; Fig. 61)*, probably in cal *AD 1430–1434 (68% probability)*. Furthermore, when the last ring of the wiggle-match is constrained to be AD 1432, the model again has good overall agreement (Acomb: 153.3, An: 20.4, n: 12), and all the radiocarbon dates have good individual agreement (A > 60).

The results from the radiocarbon wiggle-matching allow one of the two tentative matches provided by the ring-width dendrochronology to be considered as a radiocarbon-supported dendrochronological date, that spanning AD 1376–1432 (Table 15a), with the trees represented felled in the winter of AD 1432/33DR. The subscript DR indicates that this is not a date determined independently by ring-width dendrochronology, and that the master sequence, WLSKSQ01A–C, should not be utilised as a ring-width master sequence for dating other sites. The alternative tentative cross-dating for this sequence suggested by the ring-width dendrochronology, as spanning AD 1407–1463 (Table 15b) is clearly spurious, as it is incompatible with the radiocarbon wiggle-matching.

Figure 62: Map showing location of Chalk Hill, Ramsgate, Kent (image by P. Marshall).

5.7 Stratigraphy at Chalk Hill, Ramsgate, Kent

Three ditches of a causewayed enclosure, with a maximum diameter of 150m, were revealed during excavations by the Canterbury Archaeological Trust in advance of road building for Kent County Council in 1997–8 (Fig. 62; Clark et al. 2019). Thirteen segments of the inner arc, seven of the middle arc and three of the outer arc were investigated (Fig. 63). Dating of the causewayed

enclosure was undertaken in partnership with the *Gathering Time* project, funded by English Heritage and the Arts and Humanities Research Board, and based in Cardiff University (Whittle et al. 2011).

A total of 23 radiocarbon measurements were made on 21 samples, all but one from the outer ditch (Table 17)[3]. Thirteen of the samples were either of articulating groups of animal bone or carbonised residues on groups of sherds from a single vessel, and so it is unlikely that this dated material was residual (*see* §3.2.2). Two other samples are less certainly considered to be freshly deposited because of their fragility: fragments of a cattle skull (UBA-14307) and a single sherd of Neolithic Bowl preserving a carbonised residue (OxA-15391). These interpretations are critical, because they mean that the stratigraphic sequence of fills through the outer ditch should be the same as the sequence of dated samples, and so the stratigraphy can be used as prior

Figure 63: Excavations at Chalk Hill, Ramsgate, by the Canterbury Archaeological Trust in 1997–8 (© Canterbury Archaeological Trust).

3. The samples dated in Groningen were processed and measured by Accelerator Mass Spectrometry, according to the procedures set out in Aerts-Bijma et al. (1997; 2001) and van der Plicht et al. (2000). Samples processed in Oxford were dated according to the procedures described by Hedges et al. (1989) and by Bronk Ramsey et al. (2004a–b). Collagen from the bone samples dated at Belfast was extracted as described by Longin (1971), graphitised as described by Slota et al. (1987), and dated by AMS (http://www.chrono.qub.ac.uk).

The results reported there are conventional radiocarbon ages (Stuiver and Polach 1977). All three laboratories maintain continual programmes of quality assurance procedures, in addition to participation in international inter-comparisons (Scott 2003). These tests indicate no laboratory offsets and demonstrate the validity of the precision quoted. The group of replicate measurements on the carbonised residue on sherd group 265 are not statistically significantly different at the 5% significance level (Ward and Wilson 1978; Table 17).

Laboratory number	Sample reference	Material
Inner Arc		
OxA-15391	Sherd Group 10	internal carbonised residue from Neolithic bowl sherd
Outer Arc		
UBA-14304	RHAR98 (2032) F1	cattle, unspecified bone
UBA-14305	---	unspecified bone fragment
GrA-30882	Articulation 10/A	pig, proximal phalanx, of identical size and development stage to another from the same context; probably from the same foot, retaining unfused epiphysis
UBA-14306	RHAR98 (1632) F1	cattle, vertebra
OxA-15390	Sherd Group 98	internal carbonised residue from 1 large body sherd among >10 from a single Neolithic bowl
OxA-15447	Articulation 37	sheep, left humerus from among numerous bones from two animals
GrA-30880	Articulation 36	sheep, left humerus from among numerous bones from two animals
UBA-14307	RHAR97 (1530)	cattle, skull fragments
OxA-15448	Articulation 23	cattle, left astragalus, articulating with tarsal
OxA-15449	Articulation 9	cattle, right radius articulating with ulna
UBA-14310	RHAR98 (1538) 1/	human, skull
UBA-14311	RHAR98 (1538) F1	cattle, metatarsal
UBA-14309	RHAR98 (1430) F1	cattle, from articulating left tibia, astragalus, calcaneum and lateral malleolus
GrA-30888	Sherd Group 265/A	fresh, well-preserved internal carbonised residue from 1 sherd out of >15 from same Plain Bowl
OxA-15509	Sherd Group 265/B	replicate of GrA-30888
OxA-17122	Sherd Group 265/B T'=0.6; T' (5%)=6.0; v=2	replicate of GrA-30888
GrA-30885	Articulation 22	cattle, right ulna articulating with radius
GrA-30886	Articulation 20	cattle, right radius, articulating with ulna
OxA-15544	Articulation 19	cattle, right radius articulating with ulna
UBA-14312	RHAR97 (59) F65	human, vertebra
GrA-30884	Articulation 6	cattle, right humerus, articulating with radius and ulna
OxA-15543	Articulation 39	cattle, right radius, articulating with ulna

Table 17: This page and opposite.
Radiocarbon measurements and stable isotopic values from Neolithic activity at Chalk Hill, Ramsgate, Kent.

Context	Radiocarbon Age (BP)	$\delta^{13}C_{IRMS}$ (‰)	$\delta^{15}N_{IRMS}$ (‰)	C:N
Segment 3, F1056, Context 1055, the homogeneous fill of a shallow segment (total depth 0.50 to 0.26 m); from a small group of sherds clustered with two flint flakes close to northern butt	4968±33	−25.1		
Segment 1, F2034, Context 2032, fill of a pit	4968±29	−21.3	5.8	3.3
Segment 2, Context 1193, extracted from soil sample from mass of animal bone, pottery, and marine shell above initial silt	4864±27	−21.7	5.5	3.3
Segment 3, F1574, Context 1586, fill of one of the early pits, which were later joined into a single segment; partly overlying pit base, partly overlying initial silts; would have been deposited soon after the pit was dug	4885±40	−20.6		
Segment 3, F1384, Context 1632, lowest fill of an early pit	4886±37	−21.7	5.1	3.4
Segment 3, F1358, Context 1272, lowest fill of a pit truncating an undated early pit	4874±33	−27.1		
Segment 3, F1683/3013, Context 1473, lowest fill of an extensive later pit, stratified above OxA-15390	4750±32	−20.9		
from the same context as OxA-15447	4730±40	−22.4		
Segment 3, F1683/3013, Context 1530, from general fill, stratified above OxA-15447 and GrA-30880	4788±33	−20.8	5.8	3.3
Segment 5, F1667, Context 55, fill of one of the primary pits eventually joined to form segment. This layer, in which there were almost no finds, was separated by c. 0.40m of chalk rubble fill from later pits. The stratigraphic and probably temporal interval between it and a large amount of fresh, well-preserved cattle bone in Context 59, much of it articulating, at the other end of the segment makes it most unlikely that articulation 23 came from any of the same animals as the samples from that context.	4952±33	−21.6		
Segment 5, F1304, Context 1259, upper fill of an early pit	4949±33	−21.8		
Segment 5, F1318, Context 1538, mixed with animal bone in a placed deposit in later pit	4687±36	−21.7	9.2	3.4
from the same context as UBA-14310	4880±35	−21.6	5.3	3.2
Segment 5, F1318, Context 1430, from the same feature as UBA-14309 and -14310	4874±34	−22.2	5.2	3.2
Segment 5, F1672, Context 72, one of the lower fills of an early pit	4825±50	−30.9		
from the same context as GrA-30888	4867±36	−27.3		
from the same context as GrA-30888	4839±31	−27.5		
	4846±22			
Segment 5, F1298, Context 59, fill of a later pit, possibly equivalent to 1256, stratified above Sherd Group 265	4910±40	−22.4		
from the same context as GrA-30885	4935±40	−22.3		
from the same context as GrA-30885	4911±31	−20.5		
from the same context as GrA-30885	4881±34	−20.7	10.3	3.4
Segment 3, F1298, Context 1256, fill of a later pit of segment, possibly equivalent to 59, stratified above Sherd Group 265	4885±40	−22.0		
Segment 3, F1440, Context 1489, later fill of a probable feature forming south-west butt of segment	4912±31	−21.5		

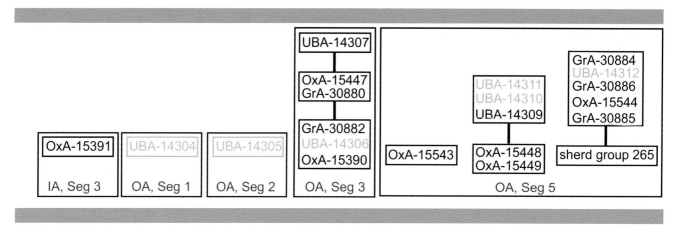

start Chalk Hill

Figure 64: Schematic diagram showing the prior information included in the chronological models for the causewayed enclosure at Chalk Hill, Ramsgate (black: freshly deposited, grey: *terminus post quem*) (image by A. Bayliss).

information for the model (Fig. 64). The status of the results on the four samples of disarticulated animal bone, and two samples of disarticulated human bone is unclear. All could be residual, although they all are short-life, single-entity samples. Although the bone dated by UBA-14305 was not identified to species, its stable isotope values are compatible with those of a terrestrial herbivore (Table 7).

All the models in this case study have been calculated in OxCal v4.4 (Bronk Ramsey 2009a) using IntCal20 (Reimer et al. 2020). They interpret all the samples as freshly deposited in their contexts, bar the six disarticulated bones, which are modelled as *termini post quos* using the AFTER function in OxCal.

Model 1 has poor overall agreement (Amodel: 56), with the dates on two samples having poor individual agreement (*sherd group 265*, A: 4 and *UBA-14310*, A: 26), both of which are slightly later than expected from their positions in the model. It is difficult to identify the cause of the problems with these dates. Sherd group 265 includes more than 15 sherds from the same Plain Bowl, and the carbonised residue was on the inside of the pot and well-preserved. There are three statistically consistent measurements on this residue, made

by two different laboratories who dated different chemical fractions of the material (the solid residue after an acid wash and multiple water rinses in Oxford, the alkali-soluble fraction from an acid-base-acid pretreatment in Groningen). UBA-14310 is from a fragment of human skull from a sub-adult/adult, possibly female, individual in what was interpreted as a placed deposit. Clark et al. (2019, 83) interpret this sample as providing the most reliable date for this context, with UBA-14311 interpreted as residual. But another date, on an articulating animal bone group from the same feature (UBA-14309) is much closer to UBA-14311 and is unlikely to be residual, although the presence of enough of the skull for age and sex to be determined suggests that it was too big to be plausibly intrusive. So perhaps UBA-14310 is slightly too young?

Since we do not know why these particular dates are problematic, we have constructed two alternative models using different forms of outlier analysis. Model 2 employs the s-type outlier model, which addresses potential underestimation of measurement uncertainty in the laboratory (Bronk Ramsey 2009b, 1037–8), and Model 3 employs the general outlier model, which is appropriate when the source of the outliers is unclear (Bronk Ramsey 2009b, 1028). In both

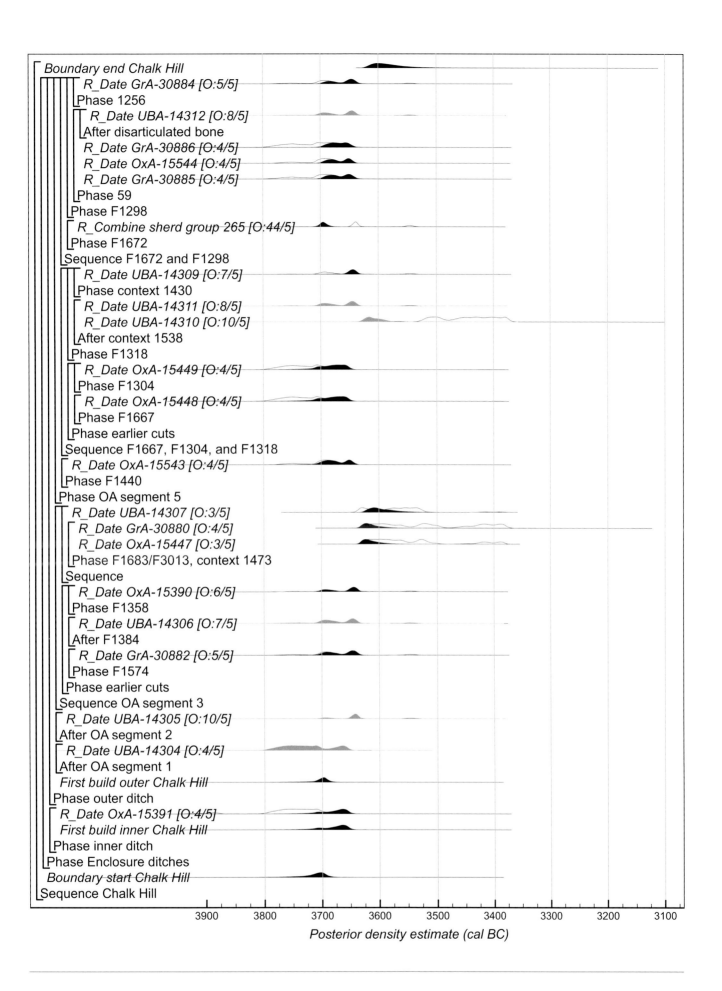

Figure 65: Probability distributions of dates from the causewayed enclosure at Chalk Hill, Ramsgate (Model 2). The format is as Figure 9 (black: fully modelled; grey: modelled as *terminus post quem;* outline: unmodelled). Posterior/prior outlier probabilities are given in square brackets. The large square brackets down the left-hand side of the diagram, along with the OxCal keywords, define the overall model exactly (image by A. Bayliss).

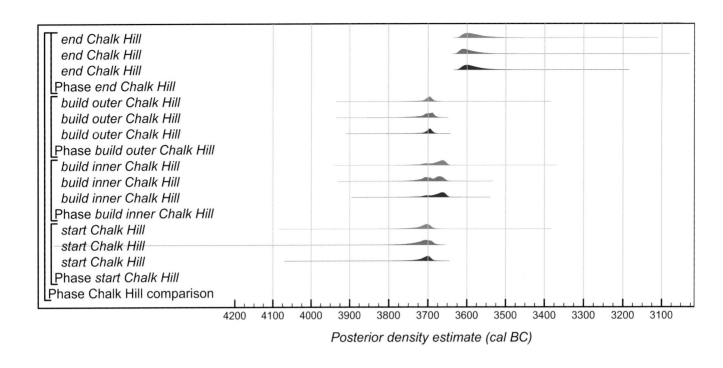

Figure 66: Graph of posterior density estimates showing key parameters for dates from the causewayed enclosure at Chalk Hill, derived from Model 1 (blue), Model 2 (orange) and Model 3 (mauve) (image by A. Bayliss).

cases, the prior probability that any result is an outlier has been set to 5%. In Model 2, three dates have posterior outlier probabilities greater than 10% (*UBA-14305*, O: 10; *UBA-14310*, O: 10; and *sherd group 265*, O: 44); and in Model 3, two dates have posterior outlier probabilities greater than this (*UBA-14310*, O: 11 and *sherd group 265*, O: 13). These dates have been down-weighted proportionally in these models.

Model 2 is illustrated in Figure 65, and key parameters from all three models are shown in Figures 66 and 67. It is clear from this sensitivity analysis that the estimated chronology for the Chalk Hill enclosure is robust against the choice

of modelling approach. The medians of the key parameters shown in Figures 66 and 67 vary by between 1 and 6 years for Models 1 and 2, and by between 3 and 16 years for all three models. Our choice of a preferred model is therefore not critical, but, given the character of the sampled material discussed above, we consider that slight under-estimation of some of the laboratory errors is the most plausible interpretation of these data and report the results of Model 2.

This suggests that the causewayed enclosure at Chalk Hill was established in *3780–3675 cal BC (95% probability; start Chalk Hill;* Fig. 65), probably in *3730–3690 cal BC (68% probability).* The outer

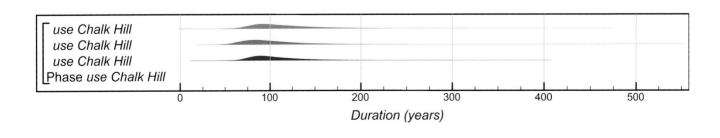

Figure 67: Probability distribution for the duration of use of the causewayed enclosure at Chalk Hill, derived from Model 1 (blue), Model 2 (orange), and Model 3 (mauve) (image by A. Bayliss).

arc was built in *3760–3675 cal BC (95% probability; build outer Chalk Hill;* Fig. 65), probably in *3715–3685 cal BC (68% probability)*. Any estimate for the inner arc is extremely tentative because it is based on a single measurement, although the model suggests that this arc was built in *3740–3645 cal BC (95% probability; build inner Chalk Hill;* Fig. 65), probably in *3710–3700 cal BC (5% probability)* or *3690–3650 cal BC (63% probability)*. In segments 3 and 5 of the outer arc, the stratigraphically latest dated samples were from close to the end of sequences of numerous recuts. The estimate for the end of use of the enclosure based on these samples is therefore close to the age of the final deposits in these segments. The model suggests that the Chalk Hill enclosure was abandoned in *3625–3510 cal BC (95% probability; end Chalk Hill;* Fig. 65), probably in *3620–3565 cal BC (68% probability)*. By comparing the modelled date estimates for the initial construction of the enclosure and its abandonment, we can suggest that the enclosure was used for *55–200 years (95% probability; use Chalk Hill;* Fig. 67 (orange)), probably for *70–135 years (68% probability)*.

Appendix: Where to get advice and information

A: Historic England

The first point of contact within Historic England for general archaeological science enquiries, including those relating to radiocarbon dating and Bayesian Chronological Modelling, should be the Historic England science advisors, who can provide independent, non-commercial advice. They are based in the Historic England local offices.

For contact details see http://www. HistoricEngland.org.uk/scienceadvice.

Specialist advice on radiocarbon dating and Bayesian Chronological Modelling can be sought from the Historic England Scientific Dating Team:

Historic England
Cannon Bridge House
25 Dowgate Hill
London EC4R 2YA

Email: c14@historicengland.org.uk
Mobile: 07584 522 333 / 07584 522 816

B. Radiocarbon dating laboratories

All radiocarbon dating laboratories will be happy to advise on the technical aspects of radiocarbon dating that effect the selection of suitable samples, on suitable storage and packaging, and on the methods of sample preparation and dating used in their facility (see §3.2.1, §3.2.3, and §3.6.1). Some will additionally be able to advise on the archaeological and statistical aspects of sample selection (see §3.2.2 and §3.3).

Laboratories put a great deal of skill and effort into dating the samples sent to them accurately, thus they welcome the opportunity to provide guidance on sample selection to ensure that together you provide the best dating possible for your samples.

A full list of radiocarbon laboratories is maintained by the journal *Radiocarbon* (http://www. radiocarbon.org/Info/Labs.pdf).

C. On-line resources

Radiocarbon datelists
An Index to Radiocarbon Dates from Great Britain and Ireland can be found at http:// www.archaeologydataservice.ac.uk/archives/ view/c14_cba. It contains basic information on more than 15,000 radiocarbon measurements. It was originally compiled by Cherry Lavell for the Council for British Archaeology, and it is comprehensive for samples from archaeological excavations until 1982, with some later additions in 1991 and 2001. Between 2007 and 2012 the index was updated with details of the measurements included in the *Gathering Time* project (Whittle et al. 2011), and with measurements funded by English Heritage before 1993.

More comprehensive details of measurements funded by Historic England (formerly English Heritage) can be found in the series of volumes of Radiocarbon Dates that are freely downloadable from https://historicengland.org.uk/images-books/publications (available as print-on-demand hard copy).

Details of many of the measurements undertaken by the Oxford Radiocarbon Accelerator Unit can be found in their on-line database at https://c14.arch. ox.ac.uk/databases.html and published in a series of datelists in the journal *Archaeometry*.

Details of the 30,517 measurements from England, Wales, Scotland, and Ireland gathered by Bevan et al. (2017) can be found at http://dx.doi.org/10.14324/000.ds.10025178.

Details of the 45,495 measurements from England, Wales, Scotland, and Ireland gathered by Bird et al. (2022) can be found at https://github.com/people3k/p3k14c.

Other datelists, particularly for measurements undertaken before c. 1980, can be found in the journal *Radiocarbon* (https://www.cambridge.org/core/journals/radiocarbon).

Calibration databases
The calibration curves that are currently internationally agreed are available from (http://intcal.org/) and the data included in them is available from (http://intcal.qub.ac.uk/intcal13/about.html).

A database of marine reservoir values is provided by the 14Chrono Centre, Queen's University, Belfast (http://calib.org/marine/).

Relevant software
A variety of freely-downloadable software is available for radiocarbon calibration, Bayesian Chronological Modelling, and dietary reconstruction. Some packages enable a wide range of models to be constructed, others are more specialised.

(a) Calibration

Calib — on-line and downloadable versions available from http://calib.org/calib/ — described in Stuiver and Reimer (1993).

IOSACal: open source radiocarbon calibration available from https://iosacal.readthedocs.io/en/latest/index.html.

MatCal — open source Bayesian ^{14}C age calibration in Matlab available from https://github.com/bryanlougheed/MatCal/ — described in Lougheed and Obrochta (2016).

rcarbon — downloadable software for the calibration and analysis of radiocarbon dates, which runs in the R software environment (http://www.r-project.org/) available from https://cran.r-project.org/web/packages/rcarbon/.

(b) Flexible Bayesian Chronological Modelling

BCal — on-line program available at http://bcal.shef.ac.uk/ — described in Buck et al. (1999).

OxCal — on-line and downloadable versions available from https://c14.arch.ox.ac.uk/OxCal; described in Bronk Ramsey (1995, 1998, 2001, 2008, 2009a–b, 2017), Bronk Ramsey et al. (2001; 2010), and Bronk Ramsey and Lee (2013).

(c) Specialist Bayesian Chronological Modelling

Bacon — downloadable package for flexible Bayesian age-depth modelling, which runs in the R software environment (http://www.r-project.org/), available from https://cran.r-project.org/web/packages/rbacon/ described in Blaauw and Christen (2011).

Bchron — downloadable package for calibration of radiocarbon dates together with routines for age-depth modelling and relative sea level rate estimation, which runs in the R software environment (http://www.r-project.org/), available from https://cloud.r-project.org/package=Bchron — described in Haslett and Parnell (2008) and Parnell and Gehrels (2015).

ChronoModel — an open source downloadable application that provides tools for constructing chronologies available from https://chronomodel.com — described in Lanos and Dufresne (2019) and Lanos and Philippe (2017; 2018).

Coffee — downloadable package that uses Bayesian methods to enforce the chronological ordering of radiocarbon dates, which runs in the R software environment (http://www.r-project.org/), available from https://cran.r-project.org/web/packages/coffee/.

(d) Classical statistical modelling

Clam — downloadable software for 'classical', non-Bayesian, age-depth modelling, available from https://cran.r-project.org/web/packages/clam/index.html — described in Blaauw (2010), which runs in the R software environment (http://www.r-project.org/).

(e) Dietary mixing models

FRUITS — downloadable software for Bayesian diet reconstruction from stable isotopic values, available from http://sourceforge.net/projects/fruits/ — described by Fernandes et al. (2014).

IsoSource — downloadable software, which calculates ranges of source proportional contributions to a mixture based on stable isotopes analysis, available from https://www.epa.gov/eco-research/stable-isotope-mixing-models-estimating-source-proportions — described by Phillips and Gregg (2003).

simmr — downloadable program for Bayesian estimation of dietary proportions from stable isotopic values, which runs in the R software environment (http://www.r-project.org/), available from https://cran.r-project.org/web/packages/simmr/ described in Parnell et al. (2010; 2013).

References

Aerts-Bijma, A. T., Meijer, H. A. J., and van der Plicht, J. 1997 'AMS sample handling in Groningen'. *Nuclear Instruments and Methods in Physics Research Section B: Beam Interactions with Materials and Atoms* 123, 221–5; https://doi.org/10.1016/S0168-583X(96)00672-6

Aerts-Bijma, A. T., van der Plicht, J., and Meijer, H. A. J. 2001 'Automatic AMS sample combustion and CO_2 collection'. *Radiocarbon* 43, 293–8; https://doi.org/10.1017/S0033822200038133

Archaeology Data Service 1997 *Guidelines for Depositors*. http://ads.ahds.ac.uk/project/userinfo/deposit.html (acc. October 2013)

Archaeology Data Service 2011 *Digital Archives from Excavation and Fieldwork: Guide to Good Practice*, 2 edn; http://ads.ahds.ac.uk/project/goodguides/excavation/) (acc. October 2013)

Archaeological Services Durham University 2019. *Arcot, Phase 1 Cramlington, Northumberland: post excavation analysis*, Report 5184; https://doi.org/10.5284/1057724

Arneborg, J., Heinemeier, J., Lynnerup, N., Nielsen, H. L., Rud, N., and Sveinbjörnsdóttir, Á. E. 1999 'Change of diet of the Greenland Vikings determined from stable carbon isotope analysis and ^{14}C dating of their bones'. *Radiocarbon*, 41, 157–68; https://doi.org/10.1017/S0033822200019512

Arnold, A. J., and Howard, R. E., 2006 *The Guildhall Complex and Pedagogue's House, Stratford upon Avon, Warwickshire, Tree-ring Analysis of Timbers*, English Heritage Centre for Archaeology Report, 68/2006; https://doi.org/10.5284/1056596

Arnold, A. J., Howard, R. E., Litton, C. D., and Dawson, G. 2005 *The Tree-ring Dating of a Number of Bellframes in Leicestershire*. English Heritage Centre for Archaeology Report, 5/2005 https://historicengland.org.uk/research/results/reports/5-2005

Arnold, A., Howard, R., Tyers, C., Bayliss, A., Bollhalder, S., and Wacker, L. 2020a *4 Walseker Lane, Harthill with Woodall, Rotherham, South Yorkshire: tree-ring analysis and radiocarbon wiggle-matching of oak timbers*. Historic England Research Report Series, 240/2020; https://doi.org/10.5284/1082553

Arnold, A., Howard, R., and Tyers, C. 2020b *41–47 High Street and the Clarence Hotel Buildings, Exeter, Devon, Tree-ring Analysis of Oak Timbers*, Historic England Research Report Series, 227/2020 https://historicengland.org.uk/research/results/reports/227-2020

Arnold, A. J., Howard, R. E., and Tyers, C., 2022 *St John The Baptist Church, Myndtown, Shropshire, Tree-ring Analysis of Timbers*. Historic England Research Report Series 43/2022

Ashmore, P. 1999 'Radiocarbon dating: avoiding errors by avoiding mixed samples'. *Antiquity*, 73, 124–30; https://doi.org/10.1017/S0003598X00087901

Association of County Archaeological Officers 1993 *Model Briefs and Specifications for Archaeological Assessments and Field Evaluations* (Bedford); https://www.algao.org.uk/sites/default/files/documents/Pubs_Model_Briefs_Specifications.pdf (acc. October 2013)

Baker, P., and Worley, P. 2019 *Animal Bones and Archaeology: recovery to archive* (Swindon) https://historicengland.org.uk/images-books/publications/animal-bones-and-archaeology/

Bayliss, A. 2007 'Bayesian Buildings: an introduction for the numerically challenged'. *Vernacular Architecture*, 38, 75–86; https://doi.org/10.1179/174962907X248074

Bayliss, A. and Harry, R. 1997 'The radiocarbon dating programme', *in* Harry, R., and Morris, C. 'Excavations on the lower terrace, site C, Tintagel island 1990–94'. *The Antiquaries Journal*, 77, 108–15; https://doi:10.1017/S000358150007517X

Bayliss, A., and Marshall, P. 2019 'Confessions of a serial polygamist: the reality of radiocarbon reproducibility in archaeological samples'. *Radiocarbon*, 61, 1143–58; https://doi.org/10.1017/RDC.2019.55

Bayliss, A., McCormac, F. G., van der Plicht, J. 2004 'An illustrated guide to measuring radiocarbon from archaeological samples'. *Physics Education*, 39, 137–44; https://doi.org/10.1088/0031-9120/39/2/001

Bayliss, A, Bronk Ramsey, C, van der Plicht, J, and Whittle, A. 2007a Bradshaw and Bayes: towards a timetable for the Neolithic. *Cambridge Archaeological Journal*, 17(suppl), 1–28; https://doi.org/10.1017/S0959774307000145

Bayliss, A., Boomer, I., Bronk Ramsey, C., Hamilton, D., and Waddington, C. 2007b 'Absolute dating', *in* Waddington, C. ed., *Mesolithic settlement in the North Sea Basin*, 65–74, (Oxford)

Bayliss, A., Hines, J., Høilund Nielsen, K., McCormac, F. G., and Scull, C. 2013 *Anglo-Saxon Graves and Grave Goods of the Sixth and Seventh Centuries AD: A Chronological Framework*, Society of Medieval Archaeology Monograph 33 (London)

Bayliss, A., Marshall, P., Dee, M., Friedrich, M., Heaton, T., and Wacker, L. 2020 'IntCal20 tree-rings: an archaeological SWOT analysis'. *Radiocarbon*, 62, 1045–78; https://doi:10.1017/RDC.2020.77

Beavan, N., and Mays, S. 2103 'The human skeleton', *in* Hines, J., and Bayliss, A., eds, *Anglo-Saxon Graves and Grave Goods of the Sixth and Seventh Centuries AD: A Chronological Framework*, Society of Medieval Archaeology Monograph 33, 101–32 (London)

Best, J., and Gent, T. 2007 'Bronze Age burnt mounds and early medieval timber structures at Town Farm Quarry, Burlescombe, Devon'. *The Archaeological Journal*, 164, 1–79; https://doi.org/10.1080/00665983.2007.11020706

Bevan, A., Colledge, S., Fuller, D., Fyfe, R., Shennan, S., and Stevens, C. 2017 'Holocene population, food production, and climate'. *Proceedings of the National Academy of Sciences*, 114, E10524-E10531; https://doi.org/10.1073/pnas.1709190114

Bird, D., Miranda, L., Vander Linden, M., Robinson, E., Bocinsky, R. K., Nicholson, C., Capriles, J. M., Gayo, E. M., Gil, A., d'Alpoim, J., Hoggarth, J. A., Kay, A., Loftus, A., Lombardo, U., Mackie, M., Palmisano, A., Solheim, S., Kelly, R. L., and Freeman, J. 2022 'p3k14c, a synthetic global database of archaeological radiocarbon dates'. *Scientific Data*, 9, 27; https://doi.org/10.1038/s41597-022-01118-7

Blaauw, M. 2010 'Methods and code for "classical" age-modelling of radiocarbon sequences'. *Quaternary Geochronology*, 5, 512–18; https://doi.org/10.1016/j.quageo.2010.01.002

Blaauw, M., and Christen, J. A. 2005 'Radiocarbon peat chronologies and environmental change'. *Applied Statistics*, 54, 805–16; https://doi.org/10.1111/j.1467-9876.2005.00516.x

Blaauw, M., and Christen, J. A. 2011 'Flexible palaeoclimate age-depth models using an autoregressive gamma process'. *Bayesian Analysis*, 6, 457–74; https://doi.org/10.1214/11-BA618

Bowman, S. 1990 *Radiocarbon dating* (London)

Bridge, M., Hurford, M., and Tyers, C. 2104 *Dauntsey House, Dauntsey, Wiltshire, Tree-ring Analysis of Timbers*, English Heritage Research Department Report Series, 62/2014

Brock F., Higham T., Bronk Ramsey C. 2010a 'Pre-screening techniques for identification of samples suitable for radiocarbon dating of poorly preserved bones'. *Journal of Archaeological Science*, 37, 855–65; https://doi.org/10.1016/j.jas.2009.11.015

Brock, F., Higham, T., Ditchfield, P., Bronk Ramsey, C. 2010b 'Current pretreatment methods for AMS radiocarbon dating at the Oxford radiocarbon accelerator unit (ORAU)'. *Radiocarbon*, 52, 103–12; https://doi.org/10.1017/S0033822200045069

Brock, F., Wood, R., Higham, T. F. G., Ditchfield, P., Bayliss, A., and Bronk Ramsey, C. 2012 'Reliability of nitrogen content (%N) and carbon:nitrogen atomic ratios (C:N) as indicators of collagen preservation suitable for radiocarbon dating'. *Radiocarbon*, 54, 879–86; https://doi.org/10.1017/S0033822200047524

Bronk Ramsey, C. 1995 'Radiocarbon calibration and analysis of stratigraphy: the OxCal program'. *Radiocarbon*, 36, 425–30; https://doi.org/10.1017/S0033822200030903

Bronk Ramsey, C. 1998 'Probability and dating'. *Radiocarbon*, 40, 461–74; https://doi.org/10.1017/S0033822200018348

Bronk Ramsey, C. 2001 'Development of the radiocarbon calibration program OxCal'. *Radiocarbon*, 43, 355–63; https://doi.org/10.1017/S0033822200038212

Bronk Ramsey, C. 2008 'Deposition models for chronological records'. *Quaternary Science Reviews*, 27, 42–60 https://doi.org/10.1016/j.quascirev.2007.01.019

Bronk Ramsey, C. 2009a 'Bayesian analysis of radiocarbon dates'. *Radiocarbon*, 51, 37–60; https://doi.org/10.1017/S0033822200033865

Bronk Ramsey, C. 2009b 'Dealing with outliers and offsets in radiocarbon dating'. *Radiocarbon*, 51, 1023–45; https://doi.org/10.1017/S0033822200034093

Bronk Ramsey, C. 2017 'Methods for summarizing radiocarbon datasets'. *Radiocarbon*, 59, 1809–33; https://doi.org/10.1017/RDC.2017.108

Bronk Ramsey, C., and Lee, S. 2013 'Recent and planned developments of the program OxCal'. *Radiocarbon*, 55, 720–30; https://doi.org/10.1017/S0033822200057878

Bronk Ramsey, C., van der Plicht, J., and Weninger, B. 2001 ' "Wiggle matching" radiocarbon dates'. *Radiocarbon*, 43, 381–9 https://doi.org/10.1017/S0033822200038248

Bronk Ramsey, C., Higham, T., and Leach, P. 2004a 'Towards high precision AMS: progress and limitations'. *Radiocarbon*, 46, 17–24; https://doi.org/10.1017/S0033822200039308

Bronk Ramsey, C., Higham, T. F., Bowles, A., and Hedges, R.E.M. 2004b 'Improvements to the pre-treatment of bone at Oxford'. *Radiocarbon* 46, 155–63; https://doi.org/10.1017/S0033822200039473

Bronk Ramsey, C., Dee, M., Lee, S., Nakagawa, T., and Staff, R. A. 2010 'Developments in the calibration and modeling of radiocarbon dates'. *Radiocarbon*, 52, 953–61; https://doi.org/10.1017/S0033822200046063

Brown, D. H. 2011 *Archaeological Archives. A Guide to Best Practice in Creation, Compilation, Transfer and Curation*, 2 edn (Reading); https://archives.archaeologyuk.org/aaf_archaeological_archives_2011.pdf (acc. August 2021).

Brunning, R., and Watson, J. 2010 *Waterlogged Wood: Guidelines on the Recording, Sampling, Conservation, and Curation of Waterlogged Wood*, (Swindon); https://historicengland.org.uk/images-books/publications/waterlogged-wood/waterlogged-wood/

Buck, C. E., Cavanagh, W. G., and Litton, C. D. 1996 *Bayesian Approach to Interpreting Archaeological Data* (Chichester)

Buck, C. E., Litton, C. D. and Smith, A. F .M. 1992 'Calibration of radiocarbon results pertaining to related archaeological events'. *Journal of Archaeological Science,*19, 497–512; http://dx.doi.org/10.1016/0305-4403(92)90025-X

Buck C. E., Christen J. A., and James, G. N. 1999 'BCal: an on- line Bayesian radiocarbon calibration tool. *Internet Archaeology*, 7; https://doi.org/10.11141/ia.7.1

Buckley, R., Morris, R., Appleby, J., King, T., O'Sullivan, D., and Foxhall, L. 2013 ' "The king in the car park": new light on the death and burial of Richard III in the Grey Friars church, Leicester, in 1485'. *Antiquity*, 87, 519–38; https://doi.org/10.1017/S0003598X00049103

Campbell, G., Moffett, L., and Straker, V. 2011 *Environmental Archaeology. A Guide to the Theory and Practice of Methods, from Sampling and Recovery to Post-excavation*, 2 edn. (Swindon); https://historicengland.org.uk/images-books/publications/environmental-archaeology-2nd/

Chartered Institute for Archaeologists 2014a *Standard and Guidance for Archaeological Excavation*. https://www.archaeologists.net/sites/default/files/CIfAS&GExcavation_1.pdf (acc. August 2021)

Chartered Institute for Archaeologists 2014b *Standard and Guidance for Archaeological Field Evaluation*. https://www.archaeologists.net/sites/default/files/CIfAS&GFieldevaluation_1.pdf (acc. August 2021)

Chartered Institute for Archaeologists 2014c *Code of Conduct*. https://www.archaeologists.net/sites/default/files/CodesofConduct.pdf (acc. August 2021)

Chartered Institute for Archaeologists 2020a *Standard and Guidance for Historic Environment Desk-based Assessment*. https://www.archaeologists.net/sites/default/files/CIfAS%26GDBA_4.pdf (acc. August 2021)

Chartered Institute for Archaeologists 2020b *Standard and Guidance for Archaeological Investigation and Recording of Standing Buildings or Structure*. https://www.archaeologists.net/sites/default/files/CIfAS%26GBuildings_3.pdf (acc. August 2021)

Chartered Institute for Archaeologists 2020c *Standard and Guidance for an Archaeological Watching Brief*. https://www.archaeologists.net/sites/default/files/CIfASGWatchingbrief.pdf (acc. August 2021)

Chartered Institute for Archaeologists 2020d *Standard and Guidance for the Collection, Documentation, Conservation and Research of Archaeological Materials*. https://www.archaeologists.net/sites/default/files/CIfAS%26GFinds_2.pdf (acc. August 2021)

Christen, J. A. 1994 'Summarizing a set of radiocarbon determinations - a robust approach'. *Applied Statistics*, 43, 489–503; https://doi.org/10.2307/2986273

Christen, J. A., and Litton, C. D. 1995 'A Bayesian approach to wiggle-matching'. *Journal of Archaeological Science*, 22, 719–25; https://doi.org/10.1016/0305-4403(95)90002-0

Christen, J. A., and Pérez, S. 2009 'A new robust statistical model for radiocarbon data'. *Radiocarbon*, 51, 1047–59; https://doi.org/10.1017/S003382220003410X

Clark, P., Shand, G., and Weekes, J. 2019 *Chalk Hill: Neolithic and Bronze Age Discoveries at Ramsgate, Kent*. (Leiden); https://www.sidestone.com/books/chalk-hill

Darvill, T., and Wainwright, G. 2009 'Stonehenge excavations 2008'. *The Antiquaries Journal*, 89, 1–19; https://doi.org/10.1017/S000358150900002X

Dee, M., and Bronk Ramsey, C. 2000 'Refinement of graphite target production at ORAU'. *Nuclear Instruments and Methods in Physics Research Section B: Beam Interactions with Materials and Atoms*, 172, 449–53; https://doi.org/10.1016/S0168-583X(00)00337-2

Dee, M., and Bronk Ramsey, C. 2014 'High-precision Bayesian modelling of samples susceptible to inbuilt age'. *Radiocarbon*, 56, 83–94; https://doi.org/10.2458/56.16685

Duller, G. 2008 *Luminescence Dating: guidelines on using luminescence dating in archaeology.* (Swindon) https://www.aber.ac.uk/en/media/departmental/dges/pdf/english_heritage_luminescence_dating.pdf

Dunbar, E., Cook, G. T., Naysmith, P., Tipney, B. G., and Xu, S. 2016 'AMS ^{14}C dating at the Scottish Universities Environmental Research Centre (SUERC) Radiocarbon Dating Laboratory'. *Radiocarbon,* 58, 9–23; https://doi.org/10.1017/RDC.2015.2

English Heritage 1998 *Dendrochronology: guidelines for producing and interpreting dendrochronological dates.* (London) https://historicengland.org.uk/images-books/publications/dendrochronology-guidelines/dendrochronology-pdf/

English Heritage 2006 *Archaeomagnetic Dating: guidelines on producing and interpreting archaeomagnetic dates* .(Swindon)

Esling, J., Howard, R. E., Laxton, R. R., Litton, C. D., and Simpson, W. G. 1989 'List 29 no 3 – Nottingham University Tree-Ring Dating Laboratory: results'. *Vernacular Architecture*, 20, 39–41; https://doi.org/10.1179/vea.1989.20.1.39

Fernandes, R. 2016 'A simple(R) model to predict the source of dietary carbon in individual consumers'. *Archaeomtery,* 58, 500–12; https://doi.org/10.1111/arcm.12193

Fernandes, R., Millard, A. R., Brabeck M., Nadeau, M-J., and Grootes, P. 2014 'Food Reconstruction Using Isotopic Transferred Signals (FRUITS): a Bayesian model for diet reconstruction'. *PLoS ONE*, 9, e87436; https://doi.org/10.1371/journal.pone.0087436

Griffiths, S., Johnston, R., May, R., McOmish, D., Marshall, P., Last, J., and Bayliss, A. 2021 'Dividing the land: time and land division in the English north Midlands and Yorkshire'. *European Journal of Archaeology,* 25, 216–37; https://doi.org/10.1017/eaa.2021.48

Harkness, D. D. 1983 'The extent of the natural ^{14}C deficiency in the coastal environment of the United Kingdom'. *Journal of the European Study Group on Physical, Chemical and Mathematical Techniques Applied to Archaeology* PACT, 8, 351–64

Hamilton, W. D. 2010 The Use of Radiocarbon and Bayesian Modelling to (Re)Write Later Iron Age Settlement Histories in East-Central Britain. PhD thesis, University of Leicester; https://ethos.bl.uk/OrderDetails.do?uin=uk.bl.ethos.529593

Haslett, J., and Parnell, A. 2008 'A simple monotone process with application to radiocarbon-dated depth chronologies'. *Applied Statistics*, 57, 399–418; https://doi.org/10.1111/j.1467-9876.2008.00623.x

Healy, F. 2012 'Chronology, corpses, ceramics, copper and lithics', *in* Allen, M. J., Gardiner, L., and Sheridan, A., eds *Is There a British Chalcolithic? People, Place and Polity in the Later 3rd Millennium.* Prehistoric Society Research Paper, 4, 144–63 and cd 21–80

Heaton, T., Köhler, P., Butzin, M., Bard, E., Reimer, R., Austin, W., Bronk Ramsey, C., Grootes, P. M., Hughen, K. A., Kromer, B., Reimer, P. J., Adkins, J., Burke, A., Cook, M. S., Olsen, J., and Skinner, L. C. 2020 'Marine20—The marine radiocarbon age calibration curve (0–55,000 cal BP)'. *Radiocarbon,* 62, 779–820; https://doi:10.1017/RDC.2020.68

Hedges, R. E. M., Bronk, C. R., and Housley, R. A. 1989 'The Oxford Accelerator Mass Spectrometry facility: technical developments in routine dating'. *Archaeometry* 31, 99–113; https://doi.org/10.1111/j.1475-4754.1989.tb01007.x

Hedges, R. E. M., Clement, J. G., Thomas, C. D. L., and O'Connell, T. C. 2007' Collagen turnover in the adult femoral mid-shaft: modelled from anthropogenic radiocarbon tracer measurements'. *American Journal of Physical Anthropology*, 133, 808–16; https://doi.org/10.1002/ajpa.20598

Hillam, J. 1984 *Tree-ring dating of timbers from Brampton Bierlow Hall, South Yorkshire*, English Heritage Ancient Monuments Laboratory Report, 4275 https://historicengland.org.uk/research/results/reports/4275

Hillam, J., and Groves, C. 1991 *Tree-ring dating of timbers from Stank Hall Barn, near Leeds, West Yorkshire*. English Heritage Ancient Monuments Laboratory Report, 19/1991 https://historicengland.org.uk/research/results/reports/19-1991

Hillam, J., and Ryder, P. F. 1980 'Tree-ring dating of vernacular buildings from Yorkshire: List 2'. *Vernacular Architecture*, 11, 23–31; https://doi.org/10.1179/vea.1980.11.1.23

Historic England 2015a *Geoarchaeology Using Earth Sciences to Understand the Archaeological Record* (Swindon) Historic England; https://historicengland.org.uk/images-books/publications/geoarchaeology-earth-sciences-to-understand-archaeological-record/heag067-geoarchaeology/ (acc. August 2021)

Historic England 2015b *Where on Earth Are We? The Role of Global Navigation Satellite Systems (GNSS) in Archaeological Field Survey.* (Swindon) Historic England; https://historicengland.org.uk/images-books/publications/where-on-earth-gnss-archaeological-field-survey/ (acc. February 2022

Historic England 2015c *Management of Research Projects in the Historic Environment: The MoRPHE Project Managers' Guide*, v 1.2. (Swindon) Historic England; https://historicengland.org.uk/images-books/publications/morphe-project-managers-guide/heag024-morphe-managers-guide/ (acc. August 2021)

Hogg, A, G., Lowe, D, J., and Hendy, C. 1987 'University of Waikato radiocarbon dates I'. *Radiocarbon* 29, 263–301; https://doi.org/10.1017/S0033822200056976

Howard, R. F., Laxton, R. R., Litton, C. D., and Simpson, W. G. 1992 'List 44 nos 11, 23 – Nottingham University Tree-Ring Dating Laboratory: results'. *Vernacular Architect,* 23, 51–6; https://doi.org/10.1179/vea.1992.23.1.44

Howard, R. E., Laxton, R. R., and Litton, C. D. 1996 *Tree-ring Analysis of Timbers from the North Aisle of St Nicholas' Church, Stanford-on-Avon, Northamptonshire.* English Heritage Ancient Monuments Laboratory Report, 27/1996; https://historicengland.org.uk/research/results/reports/27-1996

Hua, Q., Turnbull, J. C., Santos, G. M., Rakowski, A. Z., Ancapichún, S., De Pol-Holz, R., Hammer, S. J., Lehman, S. J., Levin, I., Miller, J. B., Palmer, J. G., and Turney, C. S. M. 2021 'Atmospheric radiocarbon for the period 1950–2019'. *Radiocarbon*, 1–23; https://doi.org/10.1017/RDC.2021.95

Hurford, M., Arnold, A. J., Howard, R. E., and Tyers, C. 2008 *Tree-ring Analysis of Timbers from Flore's House, High Street, Oakham, Rutland.* English Heritage Research Department Research Report Series, 94/2008; https://doi.org/10.5284/1033639

Hurford, M., Howard, R. E., and Tyers, C. 2010 *The Old House, Main Street, Norwell, Nottinghamshire, Tree-ring Analysis of Timbers.* English Heritage Research Department Research Report Series, 52/2010; https://doi.org/10.5284/1043428

Ingham, D. 2011 'Farming at Hill Field, Wilshamstead in the first millennium AD'. *Bedfordshire Archaeology*, 26, 167–236

Jay, M., Richards, M., and Marshall, P. 2019 'Radiocarbon dates and their Bayesian modelling', *in* Richards, M., Chamberlain, A., and Jay, M. eds, *The Beaker People: isotopes, mobility and diet in prehistoric Britain*. Prehistoric Society Monograph, (Oxford), 43–80

Johnson, B., and Waddington, C. 2008 'Prehistoric and Dark Age settlement remains from Cheviot Quarry, Milfield Basin, Northumberland'. *The Archaeological Journal,* 165, 107–264; https://doi.org/10.1080/00665983.2008.11020747

Jordan, D., Haddon-Reece, D., and Bayliss, A. 1994 *Radiocarbon Dates from Samples Funded by English Heritage and Dated before 1981.* (London) English Heritage; https://doi.org/10.5284/1028203

Keaveney, E. M. and Reimer, P. J. 2012 'Understanding the variability in freshwater radiocarbon reservoir offsets: a cautionary tale'. *Journal of Archaeological Science*, 39, 1306–16; https://doi.org/10.1016/j.jas.2011.12.025.

King, T., Fortes, G., Balaresque, P., Thomas, M. G., Balding, D., Delser, P. M., Neumann, R., Parson, W., Knapp, M., Walsh, S., Tonasso, L., Holt, J., Kayser, M., Appleby, J., Forster, P., Ekserdjian, D., Hofreiter, M., and Schürer, K. 2014 'Identification of the remains of King Richard III'. *Nature Communications,* 5, 5631; https://doi.org/10.1038/ncomms6631

Kinnes, I. 1979 *Round Barrows and Ring-Ditches of the British Neolithic.* British Museum Occasional Paper 7 (London)

Lanos, P., and Dufresne, P. 2019 *ChronoModel version 2.0: Software for Chronological Modelling of Archaeological Data using Bayesian Statistics.* https://chronomodel.com/

Lanos, P., and Philippe, A. 2017 'Hierarchical Bayesian modeling for combining dates in archeological context'. *Journal de la Société Française de Statistique*, 158, 72–88

Lanos, P., and Philippe, A. 2018 'Event date model: a robust Bayesian tool for chronology building'. *Communications for Statistical Applications and Methods*, 25, 131–57; https://doi:10.29220/CSAM.2018.25.2.131.

Lanting, J. N., Aerts-Bijma, A. T., and van der Plicht, J., 2001 'Dating of cremated bones'. *Radiocarbon*, 43, 249–54; https://doi.org/10.1017/S0033822200038078

Laxton, R. R., Litton, C. D., and Zainodin, H. J. 1988 'An objective method for forming a master ring-width sequence', *in* T. Hackens, T. Munaut, A. V., and Till, C., eds, *Wood and Archaeology. PACT (Strasbourg), Journal of the European Study Group on Physical, Chemical and Mathematical Techniques Applied to Archaeology, Conseil de l'Europe*, 22, 25–35

Leary, J., Darvill, T., and Field, D. 2010 *Round Mounds and Monumentality in the British Neolithic and Beyond*. Neolithic Studies Group Seminar Papers 10, (Oxford)

Leggett, P. A. 1980 'The use of tree-ring analyses in the absolute dating of historical sites and their use in the interpretation of past climatic trends'. PhD thesis CNAA, Liverpool Polytechnic

Lindley, D. V. 1991 *Making Decisions*, 2 edn. (London)

Litton, C. D., and Zainodin, H. J. 1991 'Statistical models of dendrochronology'. *Journal of Archaeological Science¸* 18, 29–40; https://doi.org/10.1016/0305-4403(91)90036-O

Longin, R. 1971 'New method of collagen extraction for radiocarbon dating'. *Nature* 230, 241–2; https://doi.org/10.1038/230241a0

Longworth, C., and Wood, B. 2000 *Standards in Action Book 3: working with archaeology.* (Cambridge)

Lougheed, B. C., and Obrochta, S. P. 2016 'MatCal: open source Bayesian ^{14}C age calibration in MatLab'. *Journal of Open Research Software*, 4, e42; http://dx.doi.org/10.5334/jors.130

Marshall, P., Darvill, T., Parker Pearson, M., and Wainwright, G. 2012 *Stonehenge, Amesbury, Wiltshire – Chronological Modelling.* English Heritage Research Report Series 1/2012 https://historicengland.org.uk/research/results/reports/1-2012

Marshall, P., Bayliss, A., Leary, J., Campbell, G., Worley, F., Bronk Ramsey, C., and Cook, G. 2013 'The Silbury chronology', in Leary, J., Field, D., and Campbell, G., eds, *Silbury Hill: the largest prehistoric mound in Europe* (Swindon), 97–116

Mays, S., Elders, J., Humphrey, L., White, W., and Marshall, P. 2013 *Science and the dead: a guide for the destructive sampling of archaeological human remains for scientific analysis.* (Swindon); https://apabe.archaeologyuk.org/pdf/Science_and_the_Dead.pdf

Ministry of Housing, Communities and Local Government 2021 *National Planning Policy Framework* .(London) https://www.gov.uk/government/publications/national-planning-policy-framework--2 (acc. August 2021)

Mook, W. G., and van der Plicht, J. 1999 'Reporting ^{14}C activities and concentrations'. *Radiocarbon*, 41, 227–40; https://doi.org/10.1017/S0033822200057106

Mook, W. G., and Waterbolk, H. T. 1985 *Radiocarbon Dating: European Science Foundation Handbook for Archaeologists 3.* (Strasbourg)

Morgan, R. 1980 'Tree-ring dates for buildings: List 1'. *Vernacular Architecture*, 11, 22; https://doi.org/10.1179/vea.1980.11.1.22

Müldner, G., and Richards, M. P. 2005 'Fast or feast: reconstructing diet in later medieval England by stable isotope analysis'. *Journal of Archaeological Science*, 32, 39–48; https://doi.org/10.1016/j.jas.2004.05.007

Museum and Galleries Commission 1992 *Standards in the Museum Care of Archaeological Collections.* (London); https://collectionstrust.org.uk/wp-content/uploads/2016/11/Standards-in-the-museum-care-of-archaeological-collections.pdf

Nayling, N. 2006 *Gorcott Hall, Warwickshire, Tree-ring Analysis of Timbers.* English Heritage Research Department Report Series, 54/2006 https://historicengland.org.uk/research/results/reports/54-2006

Needham, S., Bronk Ramsey, C., Coombs, D., Cartwright, C., and Pettitt, P. B. 1998 'An independent chronology for British Bronze Age metalwork: the results of the Oxford Radiocarbon Accelerator programme'. The *Archaeological Journal*, 154, 55–107; https://doi.org/10.1080/00665983.1997.11078784

Němec, M., Wacker, L., Hajdas, .I, and Gäggeler, H. 2010 'Alternative methods for cellulose preparation for AMS measurement'. *Radiocarbon*, 52, 1358–70; https://doi.org/10.1017/S0033822200046440

North-East Regional Research Framework for the Historic Environment 2022. https://researchframeworks.org/nerf/ (acc. February 2022) O'Connell, T. C., Kneale, C. J., Tasevska, N., and Kuhnle, G. G. C. 2012 'The diet-body offset in human nitrogen isotopic values: a controlled dietary study'. *American Journal of Physical Anthropology*, 149, 426–3; https://doi.org/10.1002/ajpa.22140

Olsen J., Heinemeier J., Hornstrup K. M., Bennike P., Thrane, H. 2012 ' "Old wood" effect in radiocarbon dating of prehistoric cremated bones?'. *Journal of Archaeological Science*, 40, 30–4; https://doi.org/10.1016/j.jas.2012.05.034

Parnell, A. C., and Gehrels, W. R. 2015 'Using chronological models in late holocene sea-level reconstructions from salt marsh sediments', in Shennan, I., Horton, B. P., and Long, A. J., eds, *Handbook of Sea Level Research* (Chichester), 500–13

Parnell, A. C., Inger, R., Bearhop S., and Jackson, A. L. 2010 'Source partitioning using stable isotopes: coping with too much variation'. *PLoS ONE*, 5, e9672; https://doi.org/10.1371/journal.pone.0009672

Parnell, A. C., Phillips, D. L., Bearhop, S., Semmens, B. X., Ward, E. J., Moore, J. W., Jackson, A. L., Grey, J., Kelly, D. J., and Inger, R. 2013 'Bayesian stable isotope mixing models'. *Environmetrics*, 24, 387–99; https://doi.org/10.1002/env.2221

Pelling, R., Campbell, G., Carruthers, W., Hunter, K., and Marshall, P. 2015 'Exploring contamination (intrusion and residuality) in the archaeobotanical record: case studies from central and southern England'. *Vegetation History and Archaeobotany*, 24, 85–99; https://doi.org/10.1007/s00334-014-0493-8

Phillips, D., and Gregg, J. W. 2003 'Source partitioning using stable isotopes: coping with too many sources'. *Oecologia*, 136, 261–9; https://doi.org/10.1007/s00442-003-1218-3

Rainbird, P., and Lichtenstein, L. 2018 'A Middle Neolithic ring ditch and settlement at King Alfred Way, Newton Poppleford'. *Proceedings of the Devon Archaeological Soc*iety, 76, 29–56

Reimer, R. W., and Reimer, P. J. 2017 'An online application for ∆R calculation'. *Radiocarbon*, 59, 1623–7; https://doi.org/10.1017/RDC.2016.117

Reimer, P. J., Austin, W. E. N., Bard, E., Bayliss, A., Blackwell, P., Bronk Ramsey, C., Butzin, M., Cheng, H., Edwards, R. L., Friedrich, M., Grootes, P. M., Guilderson, T. P., Hajdas, I., Heaton, T. J., Hogg, A. G., Hughen, K. A., Kromer, B., Manning, S. W., Muscheler, R., Palmer, J. G., Pearson, C., van der Plicht, J., Reimer, R W., Richards, D. A., Scott, E. M., Southon, J. R., Turney, C. S. M., Wacker, L., Adolphi, F., Büntgen, U., Capano, M., Fahrni, S., Fogtmann-Schultz, A., Friedrich, R., Kudsk, S., Miyake, F., Olsen, J., Reinig, F., Sakamoto, M., Sookdeo, A., and Talamo, S. 2020 'The IntCal20 Northern Hemispheric radiocarbon calibration curve (0–55 kcal BP')'. *Radiocarbon*, 62, 725–57; https://doi:10.1017/RDC.2020.41

Reynolds, P. J. 1995 'The life and death of a posthole'. *Interpreting Stratigraphy*, 5, 21–5; http://butser.org.uk/Life%20&%20Death%20of%20a%20Post-hole.pdf

Ryder, P. F. 1987 'Five South Yorkshire timber-framed houses'. *The Yorkshire Archaeological Journal*, 59, 51–79

Scott, E. M. 2003 'The third international radiocarbon intercomparison (TIRI) and the fourth international radiocarbon intercomparison (FIRI) 1990–2002: results, analyses, and conclusions'. *Radiocarbon*, 45, 135–408

Scott, E. M., Naysmith, P., and Cook, G. T. 2017 'Should archaeologists care about ^{14}C intercomparisons? Why? A summary report on SIRI'. *Radiocarbon*, 59, 1589–96; https://doi.org/10.1017/RDC.2017.12

Slota Jr, P. J., Jull, A. J. T., Linick, T. W., and Toolin, L. J. 1987 'Preparation of small samples for ^{14}C accelerator targets by catalytic reduction of CO'. *Radiocarbon* 29, 303–6; https://doi.org/10.1017/S0033822200056988

Snoeck, C., Brock, F., and Schulting, R. J. 2014 'Carbon exchanges between bone apatite and fuels during cremation: impact on radiocarbon dates'. *Radiocarbon*, 56, 591–602; https://doi.org/10.2458/56.17454

Sookdeo, A., Kromer, B., Büntgen, U., Friedrich, M., Friedrich, R., Helle, G., Pauly, M., Nievergelt, D., Reinig, F., Treydte, K., Synal, H-A., and Wacker, L. 2020 'Quality dating: a well-defined protocol implemented at ETH for high-precision ^{14}C-dates tested on late glacial wood'. *Radiocarbon*, 62, 891–99; https://doi.org/10.1017/RDC.2019.132

Speed, G. P., and Holst, M. 2018 *A1 Leeming to Barton. Death, Burial and Identity, 3000 Years of Death in the Vale of Mowbray*. Northern Archaeological Associates, Monograph Series 4; https://archaeologydataservice.ac.uk/archiveDS/archiveDownload?t=arch-3394-1/dissemination/NAA_1158_Monograph_Rpt-04_DBI.pdf

Sponheimer, M., Ryder, C. M., Fewlass, H., Smith, E.. K, Pestle, W. J., and Talamo, S. 2019 'Saving old bones: a non-destructive method for bone collagen prescreening'. *Scientific Reports*, 9, 13928; https://doi.org/10.1038/s41598-019-50443-2

Stastney, P., Scaife, R., Carretero, L. G., Whittaker, J. E., Cameron, N., Allison, E. 2021 'Modelling prehistoric topography and vegetation in the Lower Thames valley, UK: palaeoenvironmental context for wetland archaeology and evidence for Neolithic landnám from North Woolwich'. *Environmental Archaeology*; https://doi.org/10.1080/14614103.2021.1880683

Stuiver, M., and Polach, H. A. 1977 'Reporting of ^{14}C data'. *Radiocarbon*, 19, 355–63; https://doi.org/10.1017/S0033822200003672

Stuiver, M., and Reimer, P. J. 1993 'Extended ^{14}C data base and revised CALIB 3.0 ^{14}C age calibration program'. *Radiocarbon*, 35, 215–30; https://doi.org/10.1017/S0033822200013904

Synal, H. A., Stocker, M., and Suter, M. 2007 'MICADAS: a new compact radiocarbon AMS system'. *Nuclear Instruments and Methods in Physics Research Section B: Beam Interactions with Materials and Atoms*, 259, 7–13; https://doi.org/10.1016/j.nimb.2007.01.138

Taylor, R. E., and Bar-Yosef, O. 2014 *Radiocarbon dating: an archaeological perspective*, 2 edn (Walnut Creek, CA)

Telford, R. J., Heegaard, E., and Birks, H. J. B. 2004 'The intercept is a poor estimate of a calibrated radiocarbon age'. *The Holocene*, 14, 296–98; https://doi.org/10.1191%2F0959683604hl707fa

Tyers, I. 2001 'Dendrochronological analysis of timbers from Headlands Hall, Liversedge, Yorkshire', ARCUS Report 574c (unpublished)

Tyers, I. 2008 'Tree-ring analysis of timbers from 2 buildings on the Hanson House site, Syndale Road, Normanton', Dendrochronological Consultancy Report 180 (unpublished)

van der Plicht, J., Wijma, S., Aerts, A. T., Pertuisot, M. H. and Meijer, H. A. J. 2000 'Status report: the Groningen AMS facility'. *Nuclear Instruments and Methods in Physics Research Section B: Beam Interactions with Materials and Atoms* 172, 58–65 https://doi.org/10.1016/S0168-583X(00)00284-6

Van Strydonck, M., Boudin, M., and De Muldner, G. 2010 'The carbon origin of structural carbonate in bone apatite of cremated bones'. *Radiocarbon*, 52, 578–86; https://doi.org/10.1017/S0033822200045616

Vandeputte, K., Moens, L., and Dams, R. 1996 'Improved sealed-tube combustion of organic samples to CO_2 for stable isotopic analysis, radiocarbon dating and percent carbon determinations'. *Analytical Letters* 29, 2761–74; https://doi.org/10.1080/00032719608002279

Wacker, L., Němec, M., and Bourquin, J. 2010a 'A revolutionary graphitisation system: fully automated, compact and simple'. *Nuclear Instruments and Methods in Physics Research Section B: Beam Interactions with Materials and Atoms*, 268, 931–4; https://doi.org/10.1016/j.nimb.2009.10.067

Wacker, L., Bonani, G., Friedrich, M., Hajdas, I., Kromer, B., Němec, M., Ruff, M., Suter, M., Synal, H-A., and Vockenhuber, C. 2010b 'MICADAS: routine and high-precision radiocarbon dating'. *Radiocarbon*, 52, 252–62; https://doi.org/10.1017/s0033822200045288

Wacker, L., Christl, M., and Synal, H-A. 2010c 'Bats: A new tool for AMS data reduction'. *Nuclear Instruments and Methods in Physics Research Section B: Beam Interactions with Materials and Atoms*, 268, 976–9; https://doi.org/10.1016/j.nimb.2009.10.078

Wacker, L., Scott, E. M., Bayliss, A., Brown, D., Bard, E., Bollhalder, S., Friedrich, M., Capano, M., Cherkinsky, A., Chivall, D., Culleton, B. J., Dee, M. W., Friedrich, R., Hodgins, G. W. L., Hogg, A., Kennett, D. J., Knowles, T. D. J., Kuitems, M., Lange, T. E., Miyake, F., Nadeau, M-J., Nakamura, T., Naysmith, J. P., Olsen, J., Omori, T., Petchey, F., Philippsen, B., Bronk Ramsey, C., Prasad, G. V. R., Seiler, M., Southon, J., Staff, R., and Tuna, T. 2020 'Findings from an in-depth annual tree-ring radiocarbon intercomparison'. *Radiocarbon*, 62, 891–9; https://doi.org/10.1017/RDC.2020.49

Walker, K. 1990 *Guidelines for the Preparation of Excavation Archives for Long-term Storage.* (London)

Walker, M. 2012 *Quaternary Dating Methods.* (Chichester)

Walker, M. J. C., Bryant, C., Coope, G. R., Harkness, D. D., Lowe, J. J., and Scott, E. M. 2001 'Towards a radiocarbon chronology of the Late-Glacial: sample selection strategies'. *Radiocarbon*, 43, 1007–21; https://doi.org/10.1017/S0033822200041679

Ward, G. K., and Wilson, S. R. 1978 'Procedures for comparing and combining radiocarbon age determinations: a critique'. *Archaeometry*, 20, 19–31; https://doi.org/10.1111/j.1475-4754.1978.tb00208.x

Waterbolk, H. T. 1971 'Working with radiocarbon dates'. *Proceedings Prehistoric Society*, 37, 15–33; https://doi.org/10.1017/S0079497X00012548

Whittle, A., Healy, F., and Bayliss, A. 2011 *Gathering time: dating the early Neolithic enclosures of southern Britain and Ireland.* (Oxford)

Wohlfarth, B., Skog, G., Possnert, G., and Holmqvist, B. 1998 'Pitfalls in the AMS radiocarbon-dating of terrestrial macrofossils'. *Journal of Quaternary Science*, 13, 137–45; https://doi.org/10.1002/(SICI)1099-1417(199803/04)13:2%3C137::AID-JQS352%3E3.0.CO;2-6

Xu, S., Anderson, R., Bryant, C., Cook, G., Dougans, A., Freeman, S., Naysmith, P., Schnabel, C., and Scott, E. 2004 'Capabilities of the new SUERC 5MV AMS facility for ^{14}C dating'. *Radiocarbon*, 46, 59–64; https://doi.org/10.1017/S0033822200039357

Zeidler, J. A., Buck, C. E., Litton, C. D. 1998 'The integration of archaeological phase information and radiocarbon results from the Jama River Valley, Ecuador: a Bayesian approach'. *Latin American Antiquity,* 9, 135–59; https://doi.org/10.2307/971992

Glossary

Accelerator Mass Spectrometry (AMS) — counting ^{14}C atoms by accelerating carbon ions in a sample to very high speeds and then separating the ^{14}C using powerful electric charges and magnets.

Age-at-death offset — difference in age between a sample and the contemporary atmosphere, arising from the time when the carbon in the dated organism was laid down.

Agreement indices — a statistical measure employed in the OxCal software to assess the compatibility of standardised likelihoods with the prior beliefs in a model.

Apatite — a mineral form of calcium phosphate. Hydroxyapatite forms the main mineral component of bone.

Bayesian statistics — branch of statistics in which evidence about the true state of the world is expressed in terms of degrees of belief.

Bayes' theorem — express the relationship between prior and current beliefs (*see* Fig. 8).

β-particle — an electron emitted during radioactive decay.

Calcined — burnt grey/white. White fragments are preferred for radiocarbon dating.

Calibration — process of converting a radiocarbon measurement to an estimate of calendar date.

Carbon reservoirs — different stores of carbon on the Earth (e.g. the atmosphere, peat bogs).

Collagen — fibrous protein, one of the key skeletal substances.

Convergence — a diagnostic statistic that measures the stability of the solutions of a Bayesian model.

Conventional Radiocarbon Age (BP) — radiocarbon age calculated using the Libby half-life (5568±30 BP) and corrected for isotopic fractionation (Stuiver and Polach 1977).

Dated event — the event dated by a radiocarbon sample (e.g. the shedding of an antler).

Dendrochronology — tree-ring dating.

Dietary offsets — offset between the radiocarbon age of an organism and the contemporary atmosphere arising from diet.

Fraction Modern ($F^{14}C$) — ^{14}C content of a post-bomb sample in relation to the ^{14}C content of the atmosphere or ocean reservoir.

Fractionation — change in the ratio of two isotopes of a chemical element caused by the preferential loss or retention of one of them.

Freshwater reservoir effect — offset between the radiocarbon age of a sample and the contemporary atmosphere due to depleted carbon ingested from freshwater sources.

Fulvic acid — the fraction of bulk organic sediment that is soluble in acid.

Gas Proportional Counting (GPC) — counting the decay of ^{14}C atoms in a gas sample using the current induced in a high voltage chamber by the electron discharged by a decay event.

Half-life — the time required for half the atoms in a sample of radioactive material to decay.

Hard-water error — *see* freshwater reservoir effect.

Heartwood — the inner part of a tree that provides structural stability, but does not transport water or food reserves.

Highest Posterior Density interval — a range in which a certain proportion (usually 95% or 68%) of the true values of a distribution will lie.

Humic acid — the fraction of bulk sediment that is acid insoluble, and alkali soluble.

Humin — the fraction of bulk sediment that is insoluble in both acid and alkali.

Isotope — one of two or more forms of an element differing from each other in the number of neutrons present.

Liquid Scintillation Spectrometry (LSS) or Liquid Scintillation Counting (LSC) — counting the decay of ^{14}C atoms in a liquid sample using the flash of light produced by a scintillant chemical on each decay event.

Markov Chain Monte Carlo (MCMC) methods — a class of algorithms for sampling from a probability distribution.

Marine reservoir effect — offset between the radiocarbon age of a sample and the contemporary atmosphere due to carbon ingested from marine sources.

Misfits — radiocarbon dates that do not accurately reflect the age of the target event (arising from either laboratory or archaeological error). These are termed systematic offsets in the statistical literature.

Minerotrophic — plant or substrate receiving most of its nutrients and water from streams or springs.

Mixed-source calibration — calibration of a radiocarbon measurement from material that obtained its carbon from more than one reservoir, where calibration curves are mixed proportionately according to estimates of the amount of carbon in the sample deriving from each reservoir.

Offsets — systematic difference between two sets of radiocarbon measurements (e.g. contemporary samples from the terrestrial and marine biospheres).

Old-wood effect — *see* age-at-death offset.

Ombrotrophic — plant or substrate receiving all its nutrients and water from rain (rain fed).

Outlier analysis — a formal statistical method for identifying and dealing with outliers; a form of model averaging.

Outliers — the 1 in 20 radiocarbon ages whose true value lies outside the 95% range given by a measurement's quoted uncertainty.

Perfect pairs — a pair of samples of short-lived, single-entity materials from different carbon reservoirs that were freshly deposited in a context at the same time.

Posterior beliefs — our state of understanding a problem after considering new data.

Posterior density estimate — a function that describes the probability of a date occurring at a particular point in time.

Pretreatment — physical and chemical processing of a sample to remove exogenous carbon.

Prior beliefs — our state of understanding a problem before considering new data.

Probability — the chance of something happening.

Radiocarbon calibration — the process of converting a radiocarbon measurement into a distribution, or range, of possible calendrical dates, expressed as cal AD or cal BC.

Radioactive decay — the spontaneous disintegration of atoms by emission of matter and energy.

Range-finder date — single calibrated radiocarbon date used to identify the time when the activity occurred to within several centuries.

Reservoir effects — offsets between two sets of measurements on contemporary samples arising from differences in the age of different carbon reservoirs.

Sapwood — the outer part of a tree that contains living cells that transport water and store food reserves.

Sensitivity analysis — a series of alternative models that assess the changes in model outputs when the components are varied.

Single-entity sample — a sample composed of material derived from a single living organism.

Stable isotope — an isotope that does not undergo radioactive decay.

Standardised likelihoods — the data input into a Bayesian model (often calibrated radiocarbon dates).

Taphonomy — study of the routes and processes whereby material becomes part of the archaeological record.

Target event — the archaeological event a sample is intended to date (e.g. an antler pick is sampled to date the digging of the ditch in which it was found).

Total organic fraction — the chemical fraction of a bulk organic sediment that remains after the acid-soluble fraction has been removed.

Weighted mean — an average of two measurements, weighted to account for the errors on those measurements (*see* Ward and Wilson 1978).

Wiggle-matching — comparison of a series of radiocarbon dates separated by a known number of years against the calibration curve.